THE FIRST

ALSO BY STANLEY FISH

*Think Again: Contrarian Reflections on Life, Culture,
Politics, Religion, Law, and Education*

*Winning Arguments: What Works and Doesn't Work in Politics,
the Bedroom, the Courtroom, and the Classroom*

Versions of Academic Freedom: From Professionalism to Revolution

Versions of Antihumanism: Milton and Others

How to Write a Sentence: And How to Read One

The Fugitive in Flight: Faith, Liberalism, and Law in a Classic TV Show

Save the World on Your Own Time

How Milton Works

The Trouble with Principle

Professional Correctness: Literary Studies and Political Change

There's No Such Thing as Free Speech: And It's a Good Thing, Too

*Doing What Comes Naturally: Change, Rhetoric, and the
Practice of Theory in Literary and Legal Studies*

Is There a Text in This Class? The Authority of Interpretive Communities

THE FIRST

HOW TO THINK ABOUT HATE SPEECH,

CAMPUS SPEECH, RELIGIOUS SPEECH, FAKE NEWS,

POST-TRUTH, AND DONALD TRUMP

STANLEY FISH

ONE SIGNAL
PUBLISHERS

—

ATRIA

New York   London   Toronto   Sydney   New Delhi

ONE SIGNAL
PUBLISHERS

ATRIA

An Imprint of Simon & Schuster, Inc.
1230 Avenue of the Americas
New York, NY 10020

A portion of chapter 3 was adapted from an essay by the author first published in the *Chronicle of Higher Education* (2017). A portion of chapter 5 was adapted from an op-ed by the author first published in the *New York Times* (2018).

First One Signal Publishers/Atria Books hardcover edition October 2019

ONE SIGNAL PUBLISHERS and colophon are trademarks of Simon & Schuster, Inc.

For information about special discounts for bulk purchases, please contact Simon & Schuster Special Sales at 1-866-506-1949 or business@simonandschuster.com.

The Simon & Schuster Speakers Bureau can bring authors to your live event. For more information, or to book an event, contact the Simon & Schuster Speakers Bureau at 1-866-248-3049 or visit our website at www.simonspeakers.com.

Interior design by Kyoko Watanabe

Manufactured in the United States of America

1 3 5 7 9 10 8 6 4 2

Library of Congress Cataloging-in-Publication Data is available.

ISBN 978-1-9821-1524-1
ISBN 978-1-9821-1526-5 (ebook)

To the memory of Helene and Mitchel Craner,
"Imparadised in one another's arms"

CONTENTS

THE FIRST

in different practices. Rather, different practices, with their in-place definitions and goals, determine in any instance what "free speech" means. Yet even if freedom of speech is not a thing but a promissory note that can never be cashed in, it is a large and inescapable component of our political rhetoric. We are invested in it, and almost everything of note that happens is attached, sometimes by the loosest of ligatures, to free-speech issues.

Consider, for example, the last ten days of October 2018. A man named Cesar Sayoc sent pipe bombs to CNN and a dozen prominent critics of President Donald Trump. Another loner, Robert Bowers, killed eleven Jews in Pittsburgh as they prayed. Almost as soon as these events occurred, they became attached to issues of free speech. Sayoc drove, and sometimes slept in, a van plastered with pro-Trump stickers and with images of Hillary Clinton and other progressives portrayed as the targets of gunfire. Was that the mere expression of political opinion or a "true threat," a term of art that means a threat likely to be acted on? Bowers spewed anti-Semitic slogans as he went about his murderous work. Both men had online histories that identified them as haters, conspiracy theorists, and racists. Should the authorities have been alert to the danger they posed? Could they act only after Sayoc and Bowers had already acted? The digital trail was long, and the van with its disturbing images was visible on the streets of Miami for some time. Should President Trump be held to account for the anti-immigrant, anti-"other" rhetoric that, some said, made atrocities like these inevitable? Did his rantings against Hillary Clinton, George Soros, Cory Booker, Kamala Harris, Barack Obama, Eric Holder, Maxine Waters, and others make up a hit list Sayoc dutifully followed? Was Trump saying to Sayoc what Henry II said to those who promptly went out and murdered Thomas Becket: "Will no one rid me of this meddlesome priest?" Was his invective more than a dog whistle? Was it, in fact, a marching order? Was the order heeded by Coast Guard Lt. Christopher Paul Hasson when, in February 2019, he compiled a list of Democrats and anti-Trump journalists whose murder would announce the beginning of the race war he hoped to bring about? At least one prominent First Amendment theorist has posed the relevant question: "[W]e might ask when the State or political leaders may be held constitutionally responsible for encouraging private parties to punish critics. I suggest here that if the president or other officials direct, encourage, fund or covertly command attacks on their critics by private mobs of foreign powers, the First Amendment should be implicated."[1]

Mainstream commentators clucked over the possible relationship between Trump's words and these horrible deeds, but mostly they muttered "First Amendment" and said that however hateful someone's speech might be, unless it amounted to a direct incitement of violence, it was protected by the Constitution; free speech must prevail. "Free speech above all" was also the mantra of Andrew Torba, the CEO of the website Gab, Robert Bowers's favorite venue, characterized by the *New York Times* as the "last refuge for internet scoundrels." Torba often wears a green hat embroidered with the message "Make Speech Free Again." Is he a free-speech hero, bravely suffering the vituperation hurled at him by the *New York Times*? Or is he a prime example of how the promotion of unregulated free speech, proclaimed by First Amendment apostles as the cornerstone of democracy, can lead to a cascade of words that in time is corrosive of that same democracy? If Sayoc and Bowers didn't have an internet community where their views could be parroted back at them and amplified to the point where every toxic thought they entertained seemed universally shared, would the seeds of hatred perhaps not have flowered in the actions they ultimately took?

You might be surprised that actions so undeniably physical (what could be more physical than bombs and assault rifles?) turn out to be imbued with elements of speech, but as Supreme Court Justice Elena Kagan observed recently, "Speech is everywhere—a part of every human activity."[2] Everything we do sends a message and everything we say has an effect. What this means is that freedom of speech is not a discrete value. You can't carve speech out and pay homage to it in isolation from the actions from which it is inextricable. Free speech is not, despite Justice Robert Jackson's memorable pronouncement, the "fixed star in our constitutional constellation," the abiding light that will guide us through the kaleidoscope of circumstances if only we keep our eyes on it.[3] In fact, there is nothing "fixed" about free-speech doctrine at all. It's a grab bag of analogies, invented-for-the-occasion arguments, rhetorical slogans, shaky distinctions, and ad hoc exceptions to those distinctions, all combining to make it an artifact of the very politics it supposedly transcends. That's a mouthful, but what it means is that *the First Amendment is a participant in the partisan battle, a prize in the political wars, and not an apolitical oasis of principle.* That's the first thesis of this book. The second thesis is that there is nothing wrong with that. A First Amendment whose content and operations are through and through political is fully capable of doing the work we need it to do. Indeed, it may be more capable because, freed from the stringent demand of principle—the demand that freedom of speech be the rule without exception and no matter what the circumstance—the amendment can display the flexibility required to make useful sense of the many situations in which debates about speech emerge. The very malleability of the First Amendment—its lack of a hard center or of any center at all—may be its greatest recommendation.

The squishiness of the First Amendment infects it at the most basic level, the level of its prime purpose, which is, of course, to protect speech. But before we can begin to do that, we must clearly distinguish speech from action, and that turns out to be far from easy. Supreme Court First Amendment decisions have told us that flag burning is speech and that saying to a policeman, "You're a fascist," isn't.[4] If speech can be categorized as "symbolic action" (because it has an effect the state finds distressing) and action can be categorized as speech (because it sends a message the state wants to protect), isn't the distinction infinitely manipulable? How do you draw the line, and who should be authorized to draw it?

Suppose we could answer those questions and come up with a generally accepted definition of what is speech and what isn't. With that definition in place, is a citizen free to engage in speech without fear of repercussions? Not really, for there are "time, manner, and place" restrictions that limit your free-speech rights by telling you, for example, that you can't deliver your message from a truck with a loudspeaker while driving through a residential neighborhood at two in the morning. Neither, if you are a nurse, can you lobby for higher wages and better working conditions in the middle of an operation. Just the fact of having a certain job constrains your exercise of free-speech rights. How many of these restrictions are there, and is there a point when their cumulative weight is so great that free-speech rights, at least in some circumstances, have been reduced almost to nothing? Let's assume (as a hypothesis, not a fact) that those questions too have been answered and we have identified the scope of free-speech rights and a rough sense of the situations in which they can be invoked. Are we home free? Not quite, because inevitably someone will cite competing interests—the moral fabric of society or the mental health of individuals—and argue that they should outweigh the First Amendment in some contexts. In response, the strong First Amendment proponent will reaffirm the abstract principle and say that it should trump every time. But how do we think about those occasions when allowing speech to flow freely, no matter what its effects, causes harm to others? Is that harm just collateral damage, the necessary cost of doing First Amendment business? Are the eleven dead in Pittsburgh martyrs to the First Amendment? Is the First Amendment so basic a value that it must be upheld even when it appears to facilitate evil?

Must We Give Holocaust Deniers a Voice?

This last question is a perennial one and is the stuff of newspaper headlines. On July 19, 2018, the headline for the front-cover story of the *New York Daily News* was "Holocaust Deniers Deserve a Voice." That statement was made by Facebook founder and CEO Mark Zuckerberg, who in an interview on the previous day had explained why his platform would not banish Holocaust deniers and other "conspiracy pushers and hoax peddlers": "[A]s abhorrent as the content can be, I do think it comes down to the principle of giving people a voice." Zuckerberg is saying (and here he echoes a remark incorrectly attributed to Voltaire: "I disapprove of what you say, but I will defend to the death your right to say it") that however loathsome and reprehensible an idea or proposition may be, the core democratic principle of freedom of speech requires us to air it and forbids us to repress it. Even liars and defamers should be given a voice. That, as we shall see, is standard First Amendment doctrine. It goes along with a commonplace we've all heard and perhaps repeated: freedom of speech is meaningful only if its protection is extended to the worst speech imaginable.

Sounds good, but think about it. The argument that the more despicable the speech is, the more it merits protection makes sense only if we can be confident that when abhorrent views are given a place in the conversation, they will be exposed for what they are and rejected in favor of better views. Zuckerberg at first seemed to have that confidence. Reacting to some negative comments on the interview, he declared in a follow-up that "often the best way to fight offensive bad speech is with good speech." Here again he is piggybacking on the words of others (nothing wrong in that), in this case on the declaration by Supreme Court Justice Louis Brandeis that "the remedy [for harmful speech] is more speech, not enforced silence," and on the question posed eloquently by John Milton in 1644: "Who ever knew truth put to the worst in a free and open encounter?"[5] (The answer is: a great many people.) Note how Zuckerberg's phrase "offensive bad speech" lowers the stakes by diminishing the harms that speech might produce, for if the badness of a form of speech is that the speech is offensive— some people's sensibilities are ruffled—it is surely an overreaction to regulate or censor it. If that's all there is to it, what's the fuss? A little unpleasantness is a small price to pay for so important a principle. But as Anti-Defamation League CEO Jonathan Greenblatt pointed out in his response to Zuckerberg's remarks, Holocaust denial's effects are not so mild: "Holocaust denial is a willful, deliberate, and longstanding deception tactic by anti-Semites that is incontrovertibly hateful, hurtful and threatening to Jews."[6] With the word "threatening," Greenblatt challenges Zuckerberg's deflationary "offensive." These words, he is saying, do real damage; letting them out into the world and affording them space on the most powerful of social media platforms is not an innocent act whose consequence is merely someone's hurt feelings.

Zuckerberg tries to cover his flank by saying that Facebook is moving toward taking down "misinformation that is aimed at or [is] going to induce violence." But Greenblatt would no doubt reply that the anti-Semitism of which Holocaust denial is a version is always produced with a violent intention even if violence is not immediately and explicitly urged. It is hard to draw a bright line between aggressively hostile speech that is the mere voicing of opinion and aggressively hostile speech that bleeds into violence, although the effort to draw that line has been an ongoing project ever since 1859, when John Stuart Mill in *On Liberty* (the theoretical fountainhead of modern free-speech doctrine) distinguished between language vilifying corn-dealers as a class in the press—that's just talk—and rehearsing that same language "to an excited mob assembled before the house of a corn-dealer": that's intimidation. One could say, however, that this is merely the difference between slow poison and fast poison, between, for example, generations of anti-Semitic rhetoric in Germany and the explosion of Kristallnacht (November 9–10, 1938), when Jewish homes, synagogues, businesses, and hospitals were destroyed by mobs. Wouldn't it be better, perhaps, to eliminate the poison the moment you see traces of it? Bhikhu Parekh, a member of the British House of Lords, argues that discrete incidents of hate speech are "cumulatively capable of coarsening the community's sensibility, poisoning the minds of the young, weakening the norms of civility and decency and creating a situation in which it becomes common practice to ridicule, mock, malign."[7] The next step, Parekh says, is inevitable: "If anything can be *said about* a group of persons with impunity, anything can also be *done* to it." With that statement Parekh blurs the distinction between racist, anti-Semitic rhetoric and racist, anti-Semitic acts, and therefore blurs the distinction between speech and action on which the First Amendment depends. (If speech is not a distinct category, an amendment protecting it would have no object.) That would seem to be the choice: either be faithful to First Amendment principles by extending their protection to speech that leads to harm, or regulate harmful speech as if it were an action and become a First Amendment apostate.

Zuckerberg is caught in this dilemma. On the one hand, he doesn't want to censor anyone's speech, but on the other, he doesn't want his company to be a vehicle of evil effects. "There are," he explains, "two core principles at play here. There's giving people a voice. . . . Then there's keeping the community safe." "Look," he says almost plaintively, "I wanna make sure that our products are used for good." But how can he make sure of that without setting himself up as the arbiter of the good, something every tech CEO says he doesn't want to do? At times Zuckerberg puts his faith in the development of computer programs that will do the job by distinguishing mechanically between good speech and harmful speech. ("We took the time to build AI [artificial intelligence] tools.") The idea is that if we can come up with the right algorithms, they will identify what is truly harmful speech all by themselves without any input from fallible human judgment. (I will come back to this techno-fantasy in chapter 5.) At other times, however, Zuckerberg is less optimistic and says what Aristotle said in his defense of rhetoric: "People use tools for good and bad." In short, it's human nature (Zuckerberg also says that), and there's not much you can do about it. So in one moment Zuckerberg is putting his faith in technology, and in another he's throwing up his hands. A few weeks later he had apparently migrated from the giving-everyone-a-voice side, where he had originally positioned himself, to the keeping-the-community-safe side. Facebook removed pages belonging to conspiracy theorist Alex Jones and his website InfoWars because, the company announced, they violated "Community Standards," words capitalized in order, perhaps, to deflect attention from the obviously local and subjective nature of those standards. If it's Alex Jones and InfoWars this time, who is going to be next? And what happened to the flinty First Amendment warrior who only a short while ago refused to silence Holocaust deniers even though, as he pointed out, he is himself Jewish? Maybe there will be a new announcement on that front soon.

It is easy to poke fun at Zuckerberg's performance, but to be fair he is simply a walking emblem of the tensions, paradoxes, and contradictions that emerge whenever there is an attempt to draw a clear line between speech that is a genuine contribution to democratic deliberation and speech that threatens democracy's foundations. Facebook and other social media platforms are forever trying to draw that line (if only because they are under so much pressure from politicians and the media), but no such line can be drawn because, as I said earlier, the doctrine of free speech is radically unstable and infinitely elastic. It is not so much a clear principle as a rhetoric—a collection of high-sounding phrases (like "the Marketplace of Ideas") available for appropriation by anyone who can marshal them persuasively.

Here's another piece of evidence, this time in the headline of the lead story in the July 1, 2018, Sunday edition of the *New York Times*: "How Conservatives Weaponized the First Amendment."[8] No doubt some readers were surprised to see free speech characterized as a weapon in a political struggle. Isn't the right to free speech a protection against being silenced by one's political opponents? Isn't it the point of First Amendment doctrine to provide a space free of ideology and indoctrination? Don't the guarantees provided by the First Amendment ensure the participation in civic life of individuals whose voices would otherwise be drowned out? The scholars quoted in the *Times* article answer no to all these questions. Maybe in the public's mind free-speech doctrine serves these progressive purposes, but in recent decades, says one commentator, free speech "has become a sword for authoritarians, racists and misogynists, Nazis and Klansmen, pornographers and corporations buying elections."[9]

These are strong words, and I quote them not to endorse them but to underline their implication: far from being a concept that stands to the side of the fray, free speech is right in the middle of the fray, where it is wielded as a sword by all parties to a controversy: *You say* you're *for free speech, but the truth is that* we *are, so take* that! The party that succeeds in claiming the free speech label for its side is more than halfway to victory. So, for example, the moment the majority in *Citizens United v. Federal Election Commission* turned the question of regulating campaign contributions into a free-speech issue rather than a corruption issue, the case was over and the big money interests prevailed.[10] "It chills free speech" is almost always a winner, but free speech is not what wins because free speech is not an independent value. Free-speech arguments are never made in the name of the abstraction itself but in the name of some agenda to which free-speech rhetoric has been successfully attached, and when the argument is won, the victor will not be free speech but that agenda. Although it is often invoked as a principle with its own shape, freedom of speech is given shape (and content) by the partisan agents skillful enough to appropriate its vocabulary for their preferred ends. If I am right about this, many of the so-called free-speech controversies—about hate speech, campus speech, fake news, and much else—will wear a different aspect than they do when they are framed in the high-flown vocabulary we have inherited from over a century of First Amendment jurisprudence.

When Can We Speak Freely?

Let's begin by getting a few basic things straight. Freedom of speech is at once a cornerstone of democracy and a concept in law. The two often overlap, but they are not the same. Democracy means "rule by the people," and if the people, and not some dictator or theocrat or central committee, are to rule, each citizen must have the right to freely express his or her views about proposed policies and the performance of elected leaders. The idea is that those obliged to live under the laws should have a part in making them. But some of those laws, although established by democratic procedures, institute limits on what those who made them can say. You can't lie under oath (although you can lie to your spouse), and you can't shout "Fire!" in a crowded theater when there is no fire. In these and other contexts your freedom of speech is abridged for reasons the courts specify. Other laws abridge the freedom of the state either to curtail your speech or to compel it. The state cannot stop you from affirming Jesus Christ as your savior and it cannot force you to affirm Jesus Christ as your savior.

These do's and don'ts are the work of the First Amendment, which regulates speech interactions between you and your government. Insofar as there is a First Amendment right, it is a right you hold against the government's efforts to curb it; it is not a right you hold against nongovernmental actors who may wish, for a variety of reasons, to silence you. More often than not, when nongovernmental actors restrict or censor your speech, the First Amendment cannot be invoked to stop them. And even when the amendment guarantees your right to say something, it does not guarantee that you will suffer no consequences for having said it. What the law cannot do—penalize, dismiss, or exile you for speaking—can be done by your parents or your partner or your friends or your boss. Many people misunderstand this and think that the answer to the question *When can you exercise your free-speech rights without fear of penalty or retaliation?* is "Most of the time." They think of free speech as something the Constitution guarantees in almost all circumstances, as the default condition that holds except when an exception is allowed for a special reason. But in fact the reverse is true. Situations in which freedom of speech is a right unalloyed by any competing values or in-place restrictions are rare. The obvious (and perhaps the only) example is the Hyde Park corner or some equivalent "free-speech zone"—a place dedicated to the production of speech that is insulated from both seriousness and consequences: people get up on a soapbox or stand on a street corner emoting about anything or nothing; everyone has his or her say; no one is asked to do anything but listen, and even listening is not required.

It used to be that sports stadiums were also places where you could say anything that came into your head, but in recent years fans have been ushered out for using profanity or for taunting players with what amounts to "fighting words" (words intended to provoke a confrontation). In most contexts (ranting to yourself in the shower is another of the rare exceptions), speech is produced within an implicit understanding of the concerns it might be addressing, and the structure of those concerns—which could be political, economic, domestic, agricultural, educational, whatever—silently and without any fuss constrains which assertions are relevant and which irrelevant or frivolous or out of bounds. When you are at home, you refrain from saying what you're thinking because you know that frankness will come with a price—such as the unraveling of your marriage—you don't want to pay. When you are a student in a classroom, you can't insist (although you can politely request) on the topics to be discussed; if you are an instructor, you can't talk about anything you like (the syllabus and professional decorum constrain you) and you can't ridicule or berate your students. Those constraints—marked out in advance by the context—are not added to or imposed on the scene of expression; they give the scene of expression its shape. Whatever the practice you engage in, protocols of speech are always and already in place and you know, without reflection, which utterances are okay and to the point and which are not. As long as there is something at stake, as long as speech is more than noise indifferently produced, there's no such thing as free—that is, completely unfettered—speech. Speech is always attached and tied down to the pre-known situational context of utterance, and it is only *because* speech is attached and tied down that it has significance. Were speech to emerge from a void or be found in a bottle cast into the sea years ago, we could make something of it— attribute meaning to it—only by providing the context it lacked:

we ask ourselves, "What kind of person might have produced this untethered utterance?," and the answer we come up with or, more precisely, invent stabilizes and configures the communicative act.

It should now be clear how unusual is the Hyde Park corner or free-speech zone where anything and everything is freely said. In what we might call the "standard free-speech story," that scene is thought to be the norm, and scenes where free speech has been chipped away by exceptions are special and therefore always in need of justification. But in fact it is the other way around: what is special is the Hyde Park corner or any other artificially designated space where it doesn't matter what you say because when you enter it, the *ordinary* conditions of significance and consequence have been suspended. Absolutely free speech is the outlier case; constrained speech is the norm. Limitations on speech are part and parcel of any context in which speech is produced for a reason and not just for amusement. The standard story has it backward. Censorship, in the form of it-goes-without-saying restrictions on expression, is built into ordinary occasions of speech production. It might seem odd to say so, but censorship precedes free speech and is its precondition: if there were no censorship in the form of social or institutional purposes and goals that mark out what is appropriate and inappropriate to say, there would be no speech that was meaningful. All we would have is a succession of utterances without any frame telling us what we should pay attention to. One might say then, with only a slight metaphorical stretch, that meaningful speech—speech that says something and not everything— performs an act of censorship, every time. As the philosopher and cultural critic Judith Butler explains, "[N]o speech is permissible without some other speech becoming impermissible. . . . [C]ensorship is what permits speech" to have sense.[11]

By "censorship" Butler doesn't mean what we usually understand it to mean, an action taken by the state limiting the speech rights of a citizen. Her sense of censorship is more diffuse and is in line with the definition offered by Sue Curry Jansen: "[C]ensorship encompasses all socially structured prescriptions which inhibit or prohibit the dissemination of ideas, information and other messages . . . whether those obstructions are secured by political, economic, religious, or other systems of authority."[12] In short, censorship is all around us. Now one might well question the usefulness of so expansive a definition of censorship, for if everything is censorship, the word loses its critical edge; if it is the *general* condition, nothing stands opposite to it, and no one can be blamed for engaging in it. First Amendment jurisprudence *requires* that we distinguish between the restrictions on speech built into every socially organized context and the restrictions on speech imposed by government. Silencing is the result in both cases, but only governmental restrictions implicate the First Amendment. Perhaps it should be otherwise; perhaps silencings of all kinds should trigger First Amendment concerns. Many who wish to regulate hate speech think so, but that conversation must wait for the next chapter.

Roseanne Barr and First Amendment Opportunism

The proposition that the production of speech is constrained even when no state censor is at work is easy to illustrate. Do you and I have free speech in the workplace? No. Can an employer discipline or dismiss us because he doesn't like what we say or what our T-shirt says? Absolutely. Remember, freedom of speech is a right we have against government's efforts to suppress it, not a right to speak freely on any occasion without fear of repercussions. An employer has every legal right to fire you if he judges your speech or your clothing to be disruptive of the workplace or if he doesn't want his business to be associated with people who express your kind of views. You don't even have to espouse those views in the office in order to be shown the door. Some of those who marched on the alt-right side in Charlottesville were terminated when their employers learned what they had been up to. They of course had the right to demonstrate and to carry placards and shout "Jews will not replace us," but that right did not protect them from being penalized when they exercised it. A Google employee was let go in 2017 after he sent out an internal memo criticizing the company's diversity policy and suggesting that the underrepresentation of women in some job areas is the result not of intentional discrimination but of biological differences.[13] "[We don't want] harmful gender stereotypes in our workplace," said a company spokesperson defending the firing. She could say that because employers in the private sphere are generally free to determine which behaviors, including speech behaviors, they will countenance and which they will not.

Another example: It has been widely speculated that Colin Kaepernick, formerly a quarterback for the San Francisco 49ers, has been blackballed because NFL owners don't want the baggage associated with someone who performs a political act (taking a knee rather than standing with hand on heart during the playing of the national anthem) on the field. If that's true—and, given the scarcity of skilled quarterbacks, it likely is—the owners are fully within their rights and Kaepernick has no legal case to make unless it can be proven that two or more owners colluded in an effort to deprive him of his livelihood. To be sure, his gesture was political speech and the Constitution says that he cannot be prevented from making it, but any argument that he should not be penalized for doing something the Constitution protects will go nowhere. Your free-speech rights insulate you (in most cases) from government sanctions ("*Congress* shall make no law . . ."), not from sanctions issued by your employer.

That's something the comedian Roseanne Barr found out when she tweeted that Valerie Jarrett, an Obama aide, was the product of a union between the Muslim Brotherhood and the *Planet of the Apes*. Within twelve hours Barr's highly rated sitcom was canceled by ABC, and the CEO of Disney, ABC's parent company, called Jarrett to apologize. Did Barr have a right to say what she said? Yes. Did ABC have the right to take away her platform and, in effect, shut her up (although not, it turned out, on Twitter)? Yes, and the decision to do so no doubt involved a quick calculation of the constituencies the network would offend if it didn't and the constituencies it would offend if it did. Were there any free-speech/First Amendment issues involved? No. The issues were economic. Network broadcasting depends on advertising revenues, and advertisers are understandably wary of associating their brand with a controversial celebrity if only because of the prospect of boycotts. In 2017–18, as the #MeToo movement grew, some companies associated with a figure in the negative spotlight dithered while advertisers began to drop away; then they ended up pulling the plug anyway. Obviously ABC learned from the unhappy experience of its predecessors that it is usually better to cut your losses right away, for then you have a chance at least of retaining your corporate dignity and protecting your revenue.

When an incident like this one emerges—and they seem to emerge daily—there are always going to be those who cry "Free speech, free speech!" and ask "Can't Roseanne say what she likes without being penalized for it?" The answer is no, and the penalties she has endured have nothing to do with her free-speech rights, which have not been infringed at all. She did something stupid and professionally inadvisable, and it took the form of speech, but the consequences she suffered have no constitutional implications (no more than do the consequences television commentator Megyn Kelly suffered when she said it was all right to dress up in blackface on Halloween if you did it respectfully). To think otherwise is to engage in what Frederick Schauer calls "First Amendment opportunism." It occurs, he says, when some debated matter that appears "to have no special philosophical or historical affinity with the First Amendment" is nevertheless framed, at least by one of the parties, in First Amendment terms.[14] You want to do something but are blocked from doing it, or something has been done to you and the law seems to offer no redress; you're stymied, but what can you do? Well, Schauer explains, you can redescribe your cause as one touching First Amendment interests and hope that the redescription is persuasive to the courts.

Schauer cites as a successful example the argument made in 1976 by those who felt burdened by a Virginia law prohibiting the advertising of pharmaceutical prices. The prohibition was sought by independent pharmacists who feared that the aggressive advertising of deep-pocketed chains would drive them out of business. As Schauer observes, the case was really about whether the state should intervene in the free market in order to protect local interests. It became a First Amendment case because advertising (obviously an activity performed by speech) and not price controls happened to be the vehicle of the state's design. Ruling for the megastores, the majority in *Virginia State Board of Pharmacy v. Virginia Citizens Consumer Counsel, Inc.* turned an attempt to sell more toothpaste into a noble exercise of First Amendment freedom by equating the familiar phrase "free flow of ideas" with the new phrase "the free flow of commercial information."[15] Advertisers aren't trying to get your money; they're just providing information that will enable you as a consumer to make well-informed choices, and therefore massive advertising campaigns like those mounted by large corporations are "indispensable to the formation of intelligent opinions." (As if the formation of the public's intelligence were the goal advertising firms set for themselves! Are you kidding?) In dissent, Justice William Rehnquist remarked that he had always understood the First Amendment to be "an instrument to enlighten public decision-making . . . rather than the decision of a particular individual as to whether to purchase one or another kind of shampoo." Never mind; after the Court's holding, the First Amendment's protections extend to that too. And the way is open to decide, as the Court did thirty-four years later in *Citizens United*, that the "information" provided by campaign ads is just what the framers had in mind when they wrote the First Amendment.

Is There a Free-Speech Principle?

Obviously, then, First Amendment opportunism exists, but how should we regard it? Is it a practice courts should not engage in because it stretches the First Amendment beyond its proper shape? Or does the First Amendment have no proper shape and, in Schauer's words, is it nothing more than "a particular set of social, political and ideological moves that are available at a particular point in time"? Is there a core to the amendment, a baseline value or set of values from which one can fall away, or is the amendment the sum of whatever actions taken under its name have been recognized by the courts? This question will become urgent when we turn to the topic of free speech on campus, for we will find that in every dispute each party flies the flag of free speech and accuses the other party of tearing it down. If free speech is an identifiable thing, the two sides can't both be right: one party would be affirming it and the other would be undermining it. But if each party can make a plausible claim to be wearing the free-speech mantle, we must face the possibility that there is no *general* free-speech principle and that the label of free speech is applied by polemicists to speech practices that affirm the values they already hold: *This is the speech that should be uttered freely without restrictions because it says things I agree with.*

That is the conclusion reached by the law professor Larry Alexander, who for over three decades has been telling us that formal abstractions like free speech (formal because what it celebrates is not a particular assertion but assertion in general, no matter what its content) are empty vessels that acquire content when they are filled with preferences of the kind they claim to transcend. Any free-speech calculation will be made in relation to some pre-understanding of what speech is for. If you think that the point of free speech is to promote the free flow of ideas no matter what their content or effects, the fact that some forms of speech produce documentable harms will not be a sufficient reason for regulation. But if you believe that the point of free speech is to facilitate the search for truth, you will be open to the argument that lies and disinformation should be regulated because they frustrate that search. As Alexander explains, "[W]hat comes out of the process will be predetermined by what went into setting it up." It follows, he adds, that "a pure freedom of expression process is a vacuous concept. There are just different background conditions for expression each of which will lead to different substantive outcomes."[16] By "background conditions," Alexander means a definition of speech along with the specification of the purposes speech serves. Any such definition or specification will be local, context-specific, and challengeable by someone inhabiting another context who offers a different definition. This means that however speech and its purposes are characterized at a given moment, that characterization will be political and ideological through and through. The moral is one I drew earlier. The zone of free speech is not an oasis apart from political considerations; it is fashioned by political considerations and will always have a shape that is politically angled. As Yale Law professor Robert Post puts it, "[T]he search for any general free speech principle is bound to fail."[17]

Principle or Balance?

The failure to find a general free-speech principle is acknowledged whenever First Amendment jurisprudence downgrades freedom of speech to the status of a value. Principles are often described as inviolable (that's what we mean when we say "It's the principle of the thing"); if they are to be infringed, it is only in the most extreme circumstances. A value, in contrast, is one among many; therefore values can be and often are in competition, and the resolution of a conflict between them will involve calculations of probability (*If we do this, what risks do we incur?*) and the weighing of the costs of choosing one over another (*If we go with value X, how much of value Y will we sacrifice?*). The name for this weighing is "balancing." The great Judge Learned Hand tells us how it is to be done: first tote up the probable costs of allowing the troublesome speech to flourish, and then tote up the probable costs of regulating it, and go with the option that costs less.[18] A balancing calculation might have led the Seventh Circuit Court to side with the city of Skokie, Illinois, in its effort to prevent a neo-Nazi group from marching through neighborhoods populated by Holocaust survivors.[19] When the American Civil Liberties Union (ACLU) supported the marchers (who never in fact marched in Skokie), the organization lost some members, although many applauded what was termed its "principled stand." The principle is articulated by journalist Glenn Greenwald, who writes that the doctrine of freedom of speech is intended to foster "exactly those political ideas that are the most offensive, most provocative, and most designed to inspire others to act in the name of its viewpoints."[20] In short, the worse the speech and the more dangerous its effects, the more it deserves protection. No balancing allowed.

The tug-of-war between balance and principle is a general feature of life in a democracy, but it has a particularly visible form in Supreme Court cases, where free speech is often celebrated as a, if not *the*, central principle of our democracy. But in many of those same cases freedom of speech is treated as a value, an especially honored value to be sure, but one that can be set aside in certain well-defined circumstances. Here's the formula: when free-speech rights are in the mix, they can be outweighed if (1) limiting them serves a "compelling state interest" (lawyer talk for "really important") and (2) the protection of that interest requires the limitation of speech which must be (more lawyer talk) "narrowly tailored" and the "least restrictive means" of achieving the desired goal. This is a balancing test with a high bar—free-speech interests can be slighted only if the interest they clash with is held in the highest regard—but one that can be cleared, as it has been, for example, when the courts have allowed some limitations on the ability of antiabortion advocates to directly confront women entering a clinic.[21] In the balance, the vulnerability of women contemplating a legal act outweighed the unfettered exercise of free-speech rights.

What Is the First Amendment For?

If balancing goes on all the time despite the repeated invocation of principle, there is a disconnect between what we say about freedom of speech and what we do when freedom of speech issues arise. This disconnect is an inheritance from the history of free-speech jurisprudence, a history that unfolds in three stages. (The history I offer is a bit crude, but it will do for our purposes.) In the first stage, lasting from the beginning of the republic to the early decades of the twentieth century, speech could be regulated if it harbored within itself a "bad tendency" so that permitting it would constitute a threat to the public welfare. ("Bad tendency" has made a comeback in the form of demands by college students that certain words and phrases should not be said because they are *inevitably* imbued with racism or sexism or homophobia.) In stage 2, the bad tendency theory was succeeded by the "clear and present danger" test formulated by Supreme Court justices Oliver Wendell Holmes and Louis Brandeis. Where the bad tendency test assumes that the badness of some utterances is inherent—they are just bad no matter when or where they surface—the clear and present danger test is sensitive to the circumstances of utterance: the government must wait until it is apparent that a particular use of language is likely in the near future to bring about a "substantive evil" the state has a right and an obligation to prevent. The two tests measure the potential harm inflicted by both the content of speech and its likely effects. Speech considered deficient in these two ways—it says bad things and/or it does bad things—was thought not even to raise a constitutional issue; in a 1942 case, *Chaplinsky v. New Hampshire*, a famous paragraph lists the kinds of speech (obscene speech, insulting speech, fighting words, among others) the First Amendment will not protect because they are "no essential part of any exposition of ideas, and are of such slight social value as a step to truth that any benefit that may be derived from them is clearly outweighed by the social interest in order and morality."[22] The opposition between liberty—free speech for all no matter what is said and what the harm—and the interest society has in maintaining good order will structure First Amendment jurisprudence for decades to come.

Within twenty-five years, almost all of the forms of speech labeled "low value" (another term of art) by *Chaplinsky* had been brought under the constitutional umbrella. (This is the third stage.) How did that happen? It was in part the work of *New York Times v. Sullivan*, a case that rejected both content and effect tests and declared that speech is valuable in and of itself because no matter what it says or what it does, it contributes to the "uninhibited, robust and wide-open" conversation that is the lifeblood of a democracy.[23] Even false speech must be protected because falsehoods, as much as true statements, play a part in the ongoing work of the Marketplace of Ideas. Justice William Brennan declared, "Neither factual error nor defamatory content suffices to remove the constitutional shield." Indeed, the distinction between fact and falsehood is blurred, and that blurring is made official when in *Gertz v. Robert Welch* the Court declares, "Under the Constitution there is no such thing as a false idea," which doesn't mean that there are no false ideas, but that the falsity of an idea does not disqualify it from participation in the public dialogue.[24] (As I shall argue in chapter 5, it is this logic that paves the way for fake news and for the modern mantra "My opinion is as good as yours.") It is with *New York Times v. Sullivan* that freedom of speech officially becomes a principle, at least in the legal world, although it is a principle often breached just after it is invoked; in practice there have been any number of competing values—public safety, national security, the welfare of children—that captured the attention of the courts and led to restrictions of speech.

Yet, even if the rhetoric of principle is belied by what courts actually do, that rhetoric remains socially and politically strong. Many American citizens reflexively affirm the value of free expression and don't require that it be justified by reference to some other value. Strong free-speech advocates don't ask "What is the First Amendment for?" Merely to pose that question would be to imply that the rationale for the amendment is to be located in a goal prior to it. Freedom of speech, on the strong view, is a freestanding value. Yet any celebration of that value typically includes a list of the benefits free speech provides. It facilitates the search for truth, or it provides the free flow of information necessary to an informed citizenry, or it opens a space for dissent and thereby provides a counterweight to the pronouncements of entrenched authority. But if these are the goals the First Amendment helps us to realize, there must be some forms of speech that impede rather than aid their realization—speech that blocks or undermines the search for truth, speech that corrupts rather than informs the minds of citizens, speech that shuts the democratic conversation down rather than keeping it open. It follows that regulating such speech, rather than violating the First Amendment, is an act of fidelity to it. If you have any answer at all to the question "What is the First Amendment for?," you are logically committed to censorship somewhere down the line because your understanding of the amendment's purpose will lead you to regulate or suppress speech which serves to undermine that purpose. We see once again that censorship is not a violation of the First Amendment but the necessary vehicle of its implementation. The choice is never between free speech or censorship but between different paths of censorship, each of which will follow logically from an answer to the question "What is the First Amendment for?"

Of course if you have no answer to that question, if you think it wrong even to ask because freedom of speech just *is* our guiding principle no matter what, no argument for state regulation of speech, even one made in the name of a cherished interest, will sway you. But you will then have to explain why we should revere something that doesn't seem to be good for anything specific. Identifying freedom of speech as a self-justifying value unlinks it from any goal a society might think to promote. A value that admits no other measure than its own would seem to be at home only in a Hyde Park corner or some other place where talk is produced for its own sake and not for any result, good or bad, it might bring about. To be sure, strong free-speech proponents have a response to this line of reasoning: while the free exchange of ideas may not deliver an immediate payoff, in the long run it will lead to the ultimate clarification of issues that now seem muddied. ("Now we see in a glass darkly, but then face to face.")[25] That clarification, it is promised, will be the work of the Marketplace of Ideas, a concept often invoked by free-speech champions but one that is, as we shall see in the next chapter, more problematic than its proponents believe it to be.

The Two Stories of Speech

To this point the ruling assumption of the discussion has been that, all things considered, speech is a good thing. But there is another, darker story about speech, and it is told by Thomas Hobbes in his great work *Leviathan* (1651). When he first mentions speech, Hobbes praises it as the capacity that distinguishes us from the animals; it is "by the help of speech" that man's faculties "may be improved to such a height as to distinguish men from all other living creatures." While both men and animals will react to a loud noise, only men will devise plans to muffle it. But later, when Hobbes returns to the topic, he says that the same capacity of speech is what enables us to be duplicitous, deceptive, and destructive; it is by the "art of words" that some men "represent to others that which is good in the likeness of evil, and evil in the likeness of good." Speech as a category of action is thus a leading character in two narratives. In one, originated by the Pre-Socratic Sophists and popularized by Cicero and other classical humanists, speech is the deliverer of civilization, the faculty that allows us to formulate plans, recommend policies, urge actions, rise to life's challenges, and coordinate our efforts to better the human condition. The British historian Timothy Garton Ash provides a recent reformulation of this optimistic view: " '[F]reedom of information' and 'freedom of expression' enable 'us to get as close as humanly possible to the truth. . . . The more freely a wide range of alternatives is aired for any decision, the better chance we have in choosing the best course of action.' "[26] In the other, less happy narrative, speech is the medium through which we deceive our wives and husbands, manipulate our fellow citizens, betray our civic missions, and incite violence against our enemies. If those are the things the free flow of speech helps us to do, more free speech may not be what we want to encourage.

The thing about these two narratives is that they are both true, which is why we have two contrasting attitudes toward the production of speech enshrined in our laws. Some of our laws are obviously designed to increase the amount of speech available to the citizenry; others of our laws take note of the harms that speech engenders. The debates between the ACLU and the antipornography and anti–hate speech forces reflect this dual evaluation of speech which has been with us since by his word God created the world and by *his* words Cain tried to deny that he had killed Abel. Is there a way of purifying or distilling speech so that its good effects remain and the bad ones are filtered out? It has long been a project to do just that. It must be possible, many have thought, to fashion a mode of communication incapable of distortion and hostage to no parochial interests. If there were such a device and speakers tied themselves to it, they would be able to say only the thing that is true, for the linguistic resources necessary to falsehood would have been removed. If in speaking and writing you employ a language that cannot give voice to bad motives, you would yourself be truthful and honest, at least in your verbal behavior.[27]

This fantasy—and fantasy it is—has given rise to any number of projects. In the Middle Ages and early modern periods the plan was to re-create the language spoken by Adam and Eve in Eden, a language whose vocabulary, it was said, perfectly captured the essence of the things it named. In the seventeenth century John Wilkins, one of the founders of the British Royal Society, wrote *An Essay towards a Real Character and a Philosophical Language* (1668). The idea was to replace the ambiguity and redundancy of ordinary language with a finite universal set of symbols that would provide "elementary building blocks from which could be constructed the universe's every possible thing and notion." Such a language, Wilkins argued, would be free of redundancies (more than one word signifying a single thing), equivocals (words that refer to more than one thing), and metaphors (words that tell you not what a thing is but what it is like). Much later, in the twentieth century, the logical positivist Rudolf Carnap constructed a language in which "every primitive term is a physical term";[28] should you wish to speak of matters other than physical ones, you must define them in relation to those basic terms. Once again, no equivocals, no redundancies, no metaphors, and, also, no metaphysics. In the mid-twentieth century George Orwell offered a popular version of this perennial project when in "Politics and the English Language" (1946) he urged speakers and writers to purge foreign vocabularies from the English language and to limit themselves to good down-to-earth Anglo-Saxon words that refer precisely to things and not to abstractions. If we can thus purify our language, he declared, we will at the same time purify our thoughts and engage in a purified politics. (If it were only that easy!) The latest chapter in this story emerges with the internet and the hope that data freely circulated without filters or gatekeepers will eliminate misinformation and distortion because everything will be out in the open and deception will be impossible. In this utopian vision, the unregulated internet will be the true realization of the Market-place of Ideas.

Projects like these represent an effort to erase the darker of the two stories told about speech, but the effort will inevitably fail. Eliminating the human stain from the human process of conversing and proposition-making is a losing game, even if the game is given honorific names like "artificial intelligence." (More of this in chapter 5.) We're stuck with what we are and with the glories and liabilities of being speaking creatures. Speech will always be a gift with two faces: it makes possible the civilizing arts and enables the growth of individuals, but it is also the vehicle of suffering in the form of lies, slanders, and deceptions. As we saw, Mark Zuckerberg tries to sit on both sides of this fence. He wants to give everyone a voice even when some voices spew poison, and he also wants his platform to be a force for good and do no harm. Can he have it both ways? Is there a formula that allows us to regulate speech whose effects we deplore without compromising the free-speech principle we honor? That is the question that informs debates about hate speech, speech that flouts the norms of civilized society and in its strongest form threatens to undo the ties that bind us. Must we afford such speech First Amendment protection even when its malign effects are documented? Do we follow the principle that every view must have its chance to be heard to the bitter end, or is there a point at which we say "Enough!" and crank up the machinery of regulation? For answers, read on.

CHAPTER 2

Why Hate Speech Cannot Be Defined

The Liberal Paradox

In the previous chapter, I glanced briefly at the Skokie case, a particularly clear example of the tension between free-speech principles and the harms some forms of speech are likely to produce.[1] The neo-Nazi organizers of the proposed march through neighborhoods where Holocaust survivors had settled were forthright about their intentions. Frank Collin, the group's leader, boasted that his strategy was to use the First Amendment "against the Jew." He counted on the amendment as a cover for his efforts to inflict damage, a damage vividly described by one of his followers: "I hope they're terrified . . . because we're coming to get them again. I don't care if someone's mother or father or brother died in the gas chambers. The unfortunate thing is not that there were six million Jews who died. The unfortunate thing is that there were so many Jewish survivors."[2] You don't often get a statement as clear as that one: *We're going to assault a particularly vulnerable population, and the First Amendment, in which we have no independent interest (it's just the convenient vehicle of our design), is going to help us do it.*

The Seventh Circuit Court was fully aware of this strategy and acknowledged its source in an ideology that is "repugnant to the core values held generally by residents of this country and, indeed, to much of what we cherish in civilization." Nevertheless, the court ruled for Collin. How can something deemed repugnant to our core values and a threat to civilization itself be protected by our judiciary? The answer the court gives is that it can't decide First Amendment cases on the basis of its disapproval of what someone wanted to say even if the speech at issue is destructive of everything "we cherish." The court says several times that it despises what it protects: "We . . . feel compelled once again to express our repugnance at the doctrine which the appellees wish to profess publicly. Indeed, it is a source of extreme regret that . . . there would still be those who would resort to hatred and vilification of fellow human beings because of their racial backgrounds or religious beliefs." The regret is not so extreme, however, that it prevents the court from doing what it abhors to do. Why do it, then? The answer is implicit: *The First Amendment made us do it.* There could hardly be a better illustration of the puzzle presented to a regime of tolerance—a First Amendment regime—by a form of behavior whose ambition is to institute a regime of *in*tolerance extending even to the extermination ("We're coming to get them again") of those it opposes. At what point does toleration threaten to undo itself by giving aid and comfort to the virulently intolerant among us?

That question captures the liberal paradox, or the paradox of liberalism. By "liberalism" I don't mean a set of policies identified with the Elizabeth Warren wing of the Democratic Party. I mean, rather, the political principles given to us by the writings of Immanuel Kant, John Locke, J. S. Mill, Isaiah Berlin, John Rawls, and other Enlightenment thinkers. The core of that liberalism is a shift in the location of political authority from the powers that be to the individual. The top-down authority of a church or a king or a dictator is replaced by the authority established in the give-and-take of democratic deliberation engaged in by free, autonomous citizens who put all propositions to the tests of reason and evidence. Obedience to a fixed truth delivered by an unimpeachable source—the hallmark of monarchy and theocracy—gives way to an ethic of discovery in the context of which no viewpoint or policy is to be either anointed or dismissed in advance. No opinion, no matter how unpopular or despised it may be, is to be banned from the public square, for given our fallible condition—no one of us is a god or can pronounce as a god—it cannot be known which opinions will finally be validated in the fullness of time.

If these are the core tenets of liberalism (you can find a canonical account of them in Mill's *On Liberty*), it is easy to see why the First Amendment is the quintessential liberal doctrine. It codifies liberalism's unwillingness to rest in truths delivered from on high; it democratizes viewpoints and opens up a space for the emergence and development of dissent; it assures the robustness of public debate and militates against any effort by the state to cut debate off. The First Amendment also harbors the same potential for self-destruction that liberalism in general harbors: its very permissiveness, its disinclination to rule out points of view, requires it to be open to points of view which, if successful, will bring about its demise. Liberalism taken seriously is committed to the flourishing of ideas that have as their goal its undoing. Do we give those ideas a run for their money and risk the dissolution of the enterprise, or do we censor them and thus betray the enterprise? Given that liberalism teaches us to suspend our judgments about truth claims until deliberation has run its course, it cannot without contradiction suspend *that* teaching and elevate or dismiss forms of speech in advance; yet liberal regimes find themselves doing that all the time in order, they say, to save the enterprise. If it is to be a viable form of political action and not make love to its own death, liberalism must depart from the ideal it proclaims, the ideal of the absolutely free expression of ideas.

Reactions to this paradox differ. Some "bite the bullet" and accept the risk, as Oliver Wendell Holmes seemed to do when he famously declared that if dictatorial beliefs "are destined to be accepted by the dominant forces in the community, the only meaning of free speech is that they should be given their chance and have their way."[3] Others balk at this fatalism and declare that the Constitution is not a suicide pact, a sentiment that has been voiced by Abraham Lincoln, Robert Jackson, Arthur Goldberg, and Richard Posner, to name only a few. This reluctance to embrace a freedom of speech so total that it licenses destruction of itself has a source in John Milton's *Areopagitica*, often cited, along with Mill's *On Liberty*, as one of the founding documents of strong free-speech doctrine. Milton spends many paragraphs declaring that the free circulation of ideas is essential to the search for truth, but then, in a passage that has troubled his admirers, he says, *Of course I didn't mean Catholics, for "popery"* (his demeaning word for Catholicism), "as it extirpates all religions and civil supremacies, so itself should be extirpated." Because Catholicism is, in his view, an authoritarian discourse bent on shutting down all other discourses, it must itself be shut down so that the free circulation of ideas can be maintained. (For Milton censorship is essential to the search for truth.) After making this point, he underlines it with an early expression of the "we can't sign up for a suicide pact" argument: "[T]hat . . . which is impious or evil absolutely either against faith or manners no law can possibly permit that intends not to unlaw itself." In the mid-twentieth century, law professor Carl Auerbach made the same argument for regulating the speech of Communists: "By proscribing the Communist Party, Congress is not aiming at 'ideas and beliefs' or 'utterances' but at an organized movement seeking political power to crush democracy."[4] Milton believes the same of Catholicism and the *Collin* court believes it of Nazi doctrine, although it chooses to give Nazism a platform in the form of a march.

Every law announcing a regime of tolerance mimics Milton; it admits exceptions either explicitly at the outset or later, when the abyss of tolerance threatens to swallow everything up and render decision-making impossible: were nothing proscribed, you just wouldn't know where to go because everything would be indifferently authorized. No one wants to be in such a situation of paralysis, which means that no one really believes in free speech despite protestations to the contrary. What everyone believes in is a version of free speech arrived at *after* the necessary exception to it—if not Catholics, then Communists, racists, Holocaust deniers, traitors, libelers, homophobes—has been put in place and can serve as the basis for the making of discriminations. Only when there is a background assumption about what goals freedom of speech serves and what forms of speech are antithetical to those goals can distinctions be made between speech that is to be permitted and speech that is to be regulated. That is why although First Amendment jurisprudence repeatedly and obsessively pays lip service to a First Amendment principle, it is always finding and/or inventing ways to exclude from that principle forms of speech that are perceived to be wholly outside its pale. If First Amendment jurisprudence were to be true to its strongest theoretical imperative—allow everything, exclude nothing—it would have no pale. But then it would offer no ground on which anyone could come to a conclusion; there would just be an ever expanding range of views and no reason for taking any of them more seriously than any other. You can't logically value forms of speech unless you at the same time devalue others; "Let a thousand flowers bloom" won't do.

I return to a point made earlier: either freedom of speech is a communicative and expressive space made possible by the prior institution of constraints—this is what we think speech is for, and so we can't allow forms of speech that are subversive of what we think speech is for—or freedom of speech is a license to produce noise. If freedom of speech is to be a workable concept—something capable of making discriminations (like the discrimination between protected and unprotected speech)—it must have content in excess of the bare abstraction, and that content will always be politically angled. Only if politics is already *inside* the First Amendment in the form of a (contestable) definition of what speech is and what it is for can the doctrine provide the normative guidance we ask of it.

The Harm in Hate Speech

The lesson is, finally, a simple one, and I delivered it in the previous chapter: If we want to be faithful to the values free speech supports—values like the search for truth and the democratization of political debate—we must on occasion curtail speech deemed to be subversive of those same values. This is an insight Europeans and Canadians embrace, while Americans have traditionally pushed it away. Article 19 of the "Universal Declaration of Human Rights," promulgated by the United Nations in the wake of World War II, announces a principle that seems to countenance no exceptions: "Everyone has the right to freedom of opinion and expression; this right includes freedom to hold opinions without interference, and to seek, impart, and receive information and ideas through any media and regardless of frontiers."[5] But eighteen years later, in its "International Covenant on Civil and Political Rights," the United Nations is singing a somewhat different tune: "Any advocacy of national, religious, or racial hatred that constitutes incitement to discrimination, hostility or violence shall be prohibited by law."[6] Note that both documents bear in their titles words—"universal" and "international"—that claim a scope of application larger than any one country, but the introduction of forms of hatred that might justify regulation in some circumstances opens up a vista in which individual nationalities are invited to make determinations of what constitutes an exception in their localities. Article 22.2 of the "International Covenant" leaves no doubt about this when the exceptions are enumerated: "the interests of national security or public safety, the protection of public health or morals, or the protection of the rights and freedom of others." If the protection of these interests can outweigh the free-speech interest, hate speech is likely not to be tolerated or to be tolerated only after a balancing test has demonstrated that the danger to national security, public morals, and the rights of others is very small. Many nations in Europe and elsewhere follow Article 22.2 and criminalize speech that violates community standards.

There is an argument that in the United States we too are moving in that direction, although our public rhetoric continues to insist that our commitment to freedom of speech is unwavering. But even if our free-speech stance is less absolute than ritual celebrations of the First Amendment suggest it is, public rhetoric does real work, and it remains the case that U.S. courts are more likely to reason as Justices Anthony Kennedy and John Roberts do when, in opinions we shall visit later, they respond to the documentation of harms by simply citing the First Amendment and saying that as a nation we have chosen to protect hurtful speech. Both the United States, on one hand, and Europe and Canada, on the other, are engaged in the same project—"to reconcile the right to free speech with the fight against hate speech"[7]—but the legal scales will be tipped differently.

Of course, hate speech—which I know I have not yet defined,

but stay with me—need not be the object of legal regulation. Two scholars have made a strong case for the effectiveness of regulations put in place not by anti–hate speech laws but by informal and institutional practices. The authors examine workplace harassment policies (which sanction speech not because it is hateful but because it creates a hostile working environment for targeted employees), the standards employed by broadcast and cable companies, and the speech codes in force at many universities, and conclude that these are examples of "civil society restraining itself" without having the duty to do so imposed by criminal law.[8] Indeed society can "self-restrain" through the court of public opinion (always in session) without any recourse to the machinery of institutions or corporations. In May 2018, Aaron Schlossberg, a Manhattan lawyer, was in a restaurant near his office and heard a customer and a worker conversing in Spanish. Incensed, he harangued the two and others for not speaking English, and he told the manager that if he wanted to run a restaurant in Midtown Manhattan the least he could do was have his employees speak the country's language. He then said that the Spanish speakers whose presence angered him were probably undocumented, and he threatened to call Immigration and Customs Enforcement and have them thrown out of his country. He was asked to leave the restaurant, and eventually he did.[9]

The incident was filmed and the video went viral. Schlossberg's Facebook page was flooded with nasty comments; he was declared persona non grata by the managers of the building housing his office; politicians made dark noises about disbarment; we can only imagine what future clients of his, if there are any, will think. Clearly what he said was hostile and lacerating, but just as clearly it is protected speech (unless it crossed the line to become harassment and intimidation). He will therefore likely suffer no legal penalty. He is already, however, suffering other penalties; the social forces arrayed against him need not have recourse to the law in order to exact their punishment.

Should we perhaps rely on such forces and not embroil ourselves in passing hate-speech laws that may be more trouble than they are worth? The answer to that question may depend on how many Schlossbergs there are and how many people—we might call them innocent bystanders—will be made miserable and worse by the things they say or the signs and placards they carry. This is the issue raised by two of the most powerful voices on the side of hate-speech regulation, Jeremy Waldron and Catharine MacKinnon. MacKinnon is a famous (or, depending on your point of view, infamous) law professor, an antipornography activist and feminist who advocates a take-no-prisoners strategy in the battle against male domination. Waldron is an influential law professor and political theorist who argues that hate speech's most serious harm is the undermining of the dignity of its targets. By "dignity," he doesn't mean something so trivial as hurt feelings, but something much deeper. Hate speech, he says, intentionally corrodes "the social sense of assurance on which members of vulnerable minorities rely," the assurance "that they are accepted in society, as a matter of course, along with everyone else."[10] Waldron acknowledges that being accepted doesn't mean being immune from criticism; the ideas and behaviors of vulnerable minorities can be the object of negative analysis so long as analysis does not turn into an invective suggesting that members of those groups don't belong here, as Schlossberg more than suggested about people who speak Spanish in public. When that happens, and happens in a widespread way, the result is that some of our fellow citizens no longer feel able "to walk down the street without fear of insult and humiliation, to find the shops and exchanges open to [them], and to proceed with an implicit assurance of being able to interact with others without being treated as . . . pariah[s]." Waldron recalls the time when American Jews were met with signs announcing "Christians Only" (I remember walking daily past a beach resort known to have that policy) and observes that insofar as such signage was considered ordinary, "Jews would have to live and work and raise their families in a community whose public aspect was disfigured in this way." (It would be the functional equivalent of the yellow star in Nazi Germany.)

The word "disfigured" indicates the importance Waldron attaches to appearances; a well-ordered society, he contends, should have a public aspect welcoming to all. He thus departs from standard liberal thought, which always puts the adjective "mere" before "appearances," if only silently. Appearances are what you rise above and by so doing affirm an interior strength, a core being that remains intact after all the signs and the demeaning slogans have done their worst. Each of us, the story goes, has the capacity to ignore or discount the hostile images the world sometimes presents and emerge the better for it. To bring the state into the picture is to make the paternalistic assumption that people are not secure in their own identities and need external help to sustain them. "It suggests," says Nadine Strossen, past president of the ACLU, that the target of demeaning insults "doesn't have enough self-confidence, doesn't have enough critical capacity" to withstand them. "We are not diminished," she insists, "just because some bigot says something negative about us."[11] This is liberal heroism—just take the verbal blows, hold your head high, and move forward—and it is often preached, Waldron observes, by white academics who from the secure perch of a faculty appointment look out and explain to others what they should be willing and able to endure. But why, Waldron asks, is it the obligation of hate speech's victims and of no one else "to laboriously conjure up the courage to go out and try to flourish in what is now presented to them as a . . . hostile environment?"[12] As long as the message of hate and exclusion is spread by signs and placards and is blasted by the megaphones hate groups seem able to afford, the forces of hate will be abetted and reinforced by what seems to be just "in the air."

The message will be even more tangible when it is conveyed by statues and monuments. Former New Orleans mayor Mitch Landrieu makes a Waldron-like point when he explains why his city took down four displays erected to honor the Confederacy, including a statue of Robert E. Lee. His mind was made up, he reports, by a friend who invited him to look at the statue "from the perspective of an African American mother or father trying to explain to their fifth-grade daughter who Robert E. Lee is and why he stands atop our beautiful city."[13] Landrieu asks, "Can you look into that young girl's eyes and convince her that Robert E. Lee is there to encourage her?" He is insisting, with Waldron, that appearances matter. If monuments like Lee's dominate a city landscape, some people are being told that they are second-class citizens or barely citizens at all. But if all the signs are welcoming, everyone feels respected, at least on a basic level: "[T]he point of the visible self-presentation of a well-ordered society . . . is not just aesthetic; it is the conveying of an assurance to all the citizens that they can count on being treated justly."[14]

Hate Speech and Neutral Principles

But if the conveying of that assurance requires that the speech of some be curtailed by law, as Waldron and others argue, doesn't that create a *new* class of disadvantaged and marginalized citizens, those "unpopular racists and bigots and virulent Islamophobes whose beliefs are detested by those who make these laws?"[15] And isn't attacking and delegitimating those groups an infliction of the very dignitary harms you protest and wish to ameliorate? Waldron puts that question to himself and answers it somewhat impatiently: "One might as well say that laws against drinking-and-driving represent an attack on the discrete minority of drunk drivers." What Waldron means by this example but doesn't quite say is that the argument he rejects and mocks works by relativizing the positions he is at such pains to distinguish, the position of the hate-spouter and the position of the hate-spouter's victim. The two positions can be seen as equivalent only if they are emptied of the intentions that inform them—the intention on one hand to do harm and the intention on the other to avoid and make criminal the harms hate speech inflicts. If these intentions are not taken into account, the actions of the hate-speakers and of the person who would shut them down can be regarded as equivalent instances of an abstract category, the category of "voices that are being silenced." Minority voices are silenced when hate-speakers drown them out; hate-speakers' voices are silenced when their speech is regulated. What's the difference?

The difference is to be found in the intentions and the effects of each agenda: the effect of the hate-speaker's agenda is to cow, frighten, intimidate, and harass persons whose only "crime" is being black or Jewish or Muslim or female; the effect of sanctions declaring "You can't say that" is to diminish those harms. But that difference disappears if the context-specific details that make it obvious are generalized away in the rush to abstraction. That is always what happens when a discussion is ruled by the liberal mantras of equal treatment and equal respect, when the demand is for a principle that will deliver consistent judgments no matter what the viewpoints and agendas of those to whom it is applied. Anti-Semites and anti-anti-Semites? Well they're just different points of view, different ways of talking, and the First Amendment forbids the state from upholding or dismissing either of them. It is this logic, the liberal logic of neutrality toward points of view no matter what their content or effects, that Waldron challenges. He's not after an invariant principle that would generate conclusions fair to everyone, including purveyors of hate. That's the goal of every liberal theorist, but not his goal. He's after a remedy for a set of conditions he finds deplorable and wants to alter. He doesn't like the way things are, and he has a proposal for making them better, a proposal that, in his view, should not be held to the requirement that it be justified by an impartial measure.

Hate Speech and Pornography

Waldron's arguments parallel those made by the antipornography crusader Catharine MacKinnon, whose work he cites and praises. The link, as he explains, is MacKinnon's concern with "the look, the sound, and the feel of a society saturated with pornography." Pornography, writes MacKinnon, "institutionalizes a subhuman, victimized second-class status for women," and because it conditions men's view of what a woman is (she really wants it and she wants it rough), pornography "is one way that male supremacy is spread and made socially real."[16] That is to say, and Waldron says it, pornography is "a world defining imagery, imagery whose highly visible, more or less permanent, and apparently ineradicable presence makes a massive difference to the environment in which women have to lead their lives."[17] Pornography is speech whose baleful effects are equivalent to the effects of hate speech as Waldron describes them; pornography *is* hate speech.

The standard argument for protecting pornography is an equality argument: the First Amendment extends its protection equally to all forms of speech, even those that some find offensive and distressing. MacKinnon calls that "a stupid theory of equality" because it ignores the real-world *un*equal positions of those who produce pornography and those it depicts and, as she sees it, assaults. A formal equality—an equality asserted at a level above any substantive considerations—leaves material inequalities in place. While Canadian law (which MacKinnon praises) is "directed toward changing unequal social relations," U.S. law, she charges, is "indifferent to whether dominant or subordinate groups are being helped or hurt."[18] In MacKinnon's vocabulary, "indifferent" is an accusation; the law should attend to the plight of subordinate and oppressed groups. For mainstream First Amendment proponents, "indifferent" is a boast: *We don't allow ourselves to be swayed by political or social outcomes; we just follow the dictates of the First Amendment and let the political chips fall where they may.* MacKinnon and Waldron would reply that an equality regime that ignores actual inequalities enacts a politics of its own, the politics of reinforcing a status quo in which vulnerable minorities continue to be demeaned, excluded, and denied their dignity and women continue to be burdened by a culture-wide picture of themselves that invites exploitation and violence. *And it's all done by words.*

Taking the Speech Out of Hate Speech

I italicize the previous sentence because it points us to the conclusion implied by MacKinnon's and Waldron's polemics: if you want to stop hate speech, what you have to do is deny its status as speech and move it over into the category of action, for once this relocation has been effected, the abstract equality of all forms of speech is no longer assumed and a new question can be asked: not *What ideas do these words express?* but *What actions do these words perform?* What do these words *do*, and do we want it to continue to be done? Of course were we to ask that question, speech as a discrete activity limited to the realms of expression, contemplation, and deliberation would no longer exist. Rather than being distinguished from action, speech would be just another form of action liable to the monitoring and regulation action typically receives. *The question of whether speech can be distinguished from action and the question of whether there is a free-speech principle are the same question*: the specification of a principle would be possible only if the contours of speech as a separate entity had been definitively established; you can't have a principle of something that can't be identified and delimited.

To be sure, traditional First Amendment doctrine has long recognized that words can on occasion be "brigaded with action" in a way that forfeits First Amendment protection,[19] but MacKinnon goes much further; she insists that words, at least pornographic words, *are* actions, and therefore no less subject to the scrutiny of the law than physical blows. We must realize, she says, that pornography is not the representation of violence against women but the *doing* of violence against women: "Denigration [is] accomplished through meaningful symbols and communicative acts in which saying it is doing it."[20] Waldron is a bit more circumspect in his language, but in the last paragraph of his book, he declares that the malign effects he has been documenting—"assaults on the ordinary dignity" of some Americans—are not effects the law should ignore "just because they involve the power of speech."[21] Don't turn a blind eye to serious harms just because they are produced by words.

Waldron and MacKinnon are making what is known as a structural argument. A structural argument is one in which harms are attributed not to an individual who has committed a particular act but to in-place cultural conditions that inflict harms no person has specifically intended. If racist or anti-Semitic or pornographic talk saturates a society, members of the targeted groups suffer an injury (they are treated like second-class citizens) even though no one of them was singled out. Structural arguments often do not receive a serious hearing either in the courts or in the public square because the popular understanding is centered on the image of the individual who best expresses and exemplifies his individualism— his core being that persists through vicissitudes and changes—by rising above the mere surface of things and holding firm to a sense of worth that remains intact when hostile words are directed at him. Everyone, after all, encounters societal conditions that stand in the way of success: those who prosper persevere despite the obstacles put in their way. This, as I have already said, is heroism liberal-style, and it is a heroism Waldron and MacKinnon regard either as too expensive—you must spend too much of your time steeling yourself against assaults the law views as "only words"— or as too easily dismissive of the injuries minorities and women routinely suffer. If women just grit their teeth and "take it" in the name of freedom of speech, they are encouraging production of more of it, more of the words that harm them.

The Counterargument and the Marketplace of Ideas

It's easy to understand why some commentators recoil at the arguments Waldron and MacKinnon make, for they run contrary to the commonplace celebrations of freedom of speech we hear daily. In his response to Waldron, C. Edwin Baker, a stalwart free-speech advocate in the classical liberal mode, rehearses those commonplaces: "My premises," he says, are "(1) that the legitimacy of the legal order depends on it respecting people's equality and autonomy; and that (2) as a purely formal matter, the legal order only respects people's autonomy if it allows people in their speech to express their own values—no matter what those values are and irrespective of how this expressive content harms or leads to harms of other people."[22] Harms may occur, Baker acknowledges, and they may be produced by what speakers say, but respect for autonomy requires that we live with them. A state that adopts a paternalistic stance toward its citizens by shielding them from views it considers pernicious denies those citizens the dignity of being thought capable of making up their own minds. The law, especially First Amendment law, cannot, Baker insists, prefer arguably desirable outcomes (the elimination of prejudice, the diminishing of speech hostile to women) to the outcomes that follow, incidentally and not by design, from fidelity to the abstract principle of freedom of expression. Hewing to the First Amendment no matter what will have its costs, but, Baker insists, they are costs we must bear.

Baker's recital of his bottom-line premises does not so much engage Waldron's arguments as declare them out of step with a constitutional tradition that finds an early voice in *Cantwell v. Connecticut*, which he duly cites: "To persuade others to his own point of view, the pleader, as we know, resorts at times to exaggeration, to vilification . . . and even to false statement. But the people of this nation have ordained in the light of history, that, in spite of the probability of excesses and abuses, these liberties are, in the long view, essential to enlightened opinion and right opinion on the part of the citizens in a democracy."[23] But how is enlightened opinion to be engineered "in the long view"? If we rule out regulation of speech whose harmful effects we acknowledge, as Baker, like other liberal theorists, insists we must, what will do the work of winnowing the good speech from the bad?

The standard answer is the Marketplace of Ideas, which, it is said, is better suited to the making of the necessary distinctions than the biased, partial judgments of fallible and biased men and women. And what is it, and where is it? Those are hard questions. We know the origin of the concept. Justice Holmes introduced it in *Abrams v. United States*, when he declared that "the best test of truth is the power of the thought to get itself accepted in the competition of the market."[24] The Marketplace of Ideas has no physical location, but it is always open; it is the vast social and political space in which citizens try to work out their differences and fashion an arrangement that will enable them to live together peacefully, despite hugely differing opinions and values. Time is the medium of the hoped-for transformation of partiality and falsehood into truth, and we must wait for time's verdict because government, staffed by people with prejudices, agendas, and ambitions, cannot be trusted to do the job: "Freedom of speech is based in large part on a distrust of the ability of government to make the necessary distinctions, a distrust of governmental determinations of truth and falsity, an appreciation of the fallibility of political leaders, and a somewhat deeper distrust of governmental power in a more general sense."[25] The Marketplace of Ideas enacts liberalism's suspicion of received authority by ensuring that decisions about which speech is good and which bad are deferred until a judgment more impartial than any a political agent could be trusted to deliver emerges.

But those who argue for the regulation of hate speech aren't interested in the "long game" presided over by the Marketplace of Ideas. They are concerned with wrongs and harms that are occurring *now* and they seek remedies that can be applied in the present. The remedy they propose—regulating speech that inflicts a "dignity harm" on minorities and women—has the effect, as I observed earlier, of undermining the distinction between speech and action, a distinction presupposed by the very fact of the First Amendment. Were speech and action the same thing, the First Amendment would be saying that Congress shall make no law abridging the freedom of action, but that would amount to saying that Congress shall make no laws, for regulating action is what legislatures and courts do by definition. Even if the line between speech and action cannot be drawn as a matter of principle, the line must be drawn if we are to have any doctrine of free speech at all. The distinction may finally be theoretically indefensible, but we can't do without it. Along with the distinction comes a characterization of speech as an expressive act that stops short of the waters of action. Speech informs, announces, pronounces, entreats, explains, argues, petitions, criticizes, praises, complains, rejoices, etc.; its effects are confined to the ears and minds of those who receive it. The commonplace that captures the supposedly limited scope of speech's impact is "That's just talk," and the proverb we hear from the early days of childhood is "Sticks and stones may break my bones, but names will never hurt me."

But long before law professor Richard Delgado wrote an essay titled "Words That Wound" everyone knew that the proverb is false and that language can be made into a weapon, can be lacerating, terrifying, hurtful.[26] (It can also be uplifting: at the end of the movie *Darkest Hour*, someone says of a famous Winston Churchill speech, "He has mobilized the English language and sent it into battle."[27]) Much of the time we are able to shrug off the slights we experience when people aim verbal jabs at us; we let them "roll off our backs." But some grenades made of words are not so easily ignored; we experience them as violations, as assaults on our basic dignity, even as the denial of our humanity.

Hate Speech Finally Defined

The question—it has been the question since the beginning of this chapter—is *Should we regulate those assaults as other Western democracies do?* But the question cannot be answered until a prior question is posed, *What is hate speech anyway?*, and *that* question cannot be answered because hate speech is an unstable category. It is unstable because there is no agreement on which utterances belong in it. Only if there were a set of utterances that would be recognized by everyone as hate speech would the designation name something conceptually coherent. Although legal theorists engage in sophisticated discussions of what hate speech exactly is, there is really nothing theoretical to say about it because there is no algorithm that can pick out what is hateful from what is not. Whether something is or is not considered hate speech will be determined not by a checklist of features but by the felt experience of someone who feels deeply wounded by words that have been uttered by someone else.

But of course the producers of those words don't regard them as hateful; they regard them as truthful; they think of themselves as delivering a message the world needs to hear. The sincerity of so-called hate-speakers must be assumed; to deny it in advance is to cheat and make the game too easy to win. When members of the Westboro Baptist Church tell mourners that their sons died because America's toleration of homosexuals has angered God, they really believe it, and they also believe that if the country does not change its ways, God will send down more afflictions, as he did when the pharaoh of Egypt defied him.[28] Hate speech is often defined as the irrational expression of hatred directed at a particular group of people. The definition presupposes what has not been proven, that those who traffic in so-called hate speech have no good reasons for the prejudices (not the word they would use) they give voice to. But members of the Westboro Baptist Church think, indeed *know* that they have good reasons and that any challenge to those reasons will come not from Reason with a capital R but from reasons that flow from someone else's prejudices. The conclusion may be distressing, but it is inescapable: *hate speech is rational* even when the rationality is one you find abhorrent; it is an expression of ideas, not a physical effusion like a belch. In *Cohen v. California*, Justice John Marshall Harlan famously said, "[O]ne man's vulgarity is another man's lyric."[29] It could just as well be said that one man's hate speech is another man's (or woman's) speaking of truth to a world that needs to hear it. Only if the content of hate speech were self-identifying—if upon hearing an instance of it, a *universal* chorus would exclaim in unison, "That's hateful"—would it stand still long enough to become the object of principled regulation. But if it is a moving target, as the endless, inconclusive discussions of it amply show, any regulation of it—or of what some persons take "it" to be—will be ad hoc and political.

In the end, then, hate speech can be defined only as speech produced by persons whose ideas and viewpoints you despise and fear. *Hate speech is what your enemy says loudly*, and if you are lucky enough to prevail in an election, you may be able to get your enemy's speech labeled "hateful." But when political fortunes turn (as they always will), your enemies will then do to you and your speech what you have done to them. Because hate speech is not a thing—you can't point to it as you can point to a chair—there is nothing to be done about it that is not an exercise of political power, an exercise directed at a form of speech a current majority dislikes and fears. Any regulation of hate speech will be political, and *non*regulation of hate speech will be political too because it will give a governmental imprimatur to words whose harmful effects some citizens will suffer and seek to proscribe by law.

There is another view that has always had some currency: hate speech and the attitudes that impel it are evidence of an illness; haters and hate-speakers suffer from an abnormality that could possibly be cured by therapy or even by a pill.[30] This medicalization of a form of behavior many find distressing has the advantage, apparently, of removing the issue from the slippery realm of politics and assigning it to science. I say "apparently" because the act of designating a viewpoint as evidence of mental imbalance is a supremely political one: institutions wearing the mantle of authority just declare that a particular way of thinking is outside the bounds of rationality and is to be classified as a disease. The medicalization argument is just politics in disguise.

This is not a fatal criticism. In fact, it is not a criticism at all and would be one only if there were an alternative to politics, if hate-speech regulations could be justified *in principle*. Since they cannot be, the opposition is not between principle and politics but between political arguments that prove persuasive to the relevant constituencies and political arguments that don't. And what makes an argument persuasive? The answer, oddly enough, is that a persuasive argument for the regulation of hate speech will be one dressed in the vocabulary of principle. While the search for a principled definition of hate speech will always fail (for the same reason that the search for a principled distinction between speech and action will always fail), the *rhetoric* of principle is available as a resource for argument. It is a political fact that you can't say *I want to ban this stuff because my friends and I deplore it*; that argument won't go anywhere. But if you manage to clothe your desire to ban speech you dislike in words that breathe principle, that bit of cross-dressing might just do the trick. While the claim of principle can never be cashed out, the language of principle is necessary to the efforts of those who seek to impose regulations. Even though there are no principles in sight, you just might manage to fashion an argument made up of "principle-talk" that wins the day.

Why Attempts to Codify Hate Speech Will Always Fail

There are many who would regard what I have just said as cynical; they remain committed to finding a formula for first identifying and then quarantining hate speech. Typically, their strategy is to come up with a definition of hate speech so general that persons of every political and cultural persuasion will agree to it, and the way to do that (if it can be done) is to identify utterances so horrible that no one can find anything redeeming about them. If we could all just agree on a minimalist definition of hate speech, we might get somewhere and bring everybody along by degrees. So, for example, Viktor Mayer-Schönberger and Teree E. Foster propose a test based on the idea of *jus cogens*, the overriding principles of international law. These principles follow, they explain, from "an overwhelmingly broad consensus concerning which . . . messages entail ideas that are wholly intolerable, and thus, could be regulated."[31] Messages that might be regulated, according to Mayer-Schönberger and Foster, include those tending to endorse or advocate piracy, slavery, genocide, systematic racial discrimination, and torture. The rationale is simple: "When a speaker advocates behavior so horrifying that its dubious value is undeniably outweighed by the peril to social structure and order, a legislature should be entitled to prohibit the communication." (This is *Chaplinsky* all over again.)

"Undeniably" is the word that makes the strong and, I think, vulnerable claim. Is it really the case that no one disagrees about the "dubious value" of the activities on Mayer-Schönberger and Foster's list? Famed lawyer Alan Dershowitz has argued that under certain conditions torture is warranted and should find a place (hedged around by qualifications and procedural requirements) in our legal system. Should his essays and the message they deliver be prohibited? Mayer-Schönberger and Foster admit there will be dissenters—individuals like Dershowitz and entire states advocating actions the majority of us find "horrifying"—but insist "that a handful of objectors cannot obstruct the establishment of a *jus cogens* rule." Why "cannot"? Because those of us in the mainstream will outnumber them; there's the handful, and there's the rest of us. The category of speech so awful that the state is justified in prohibiting it will be filled in by majority vote, exactly what John Stuart Mill inveighed against when he famously declared, "If all mankind minus one were of one opinion and only one person were of the contrary opinion, mankind would be no more justified in silencing that one person than he, if he had the power, would be justified in silencing mankind."[32] Mill sees clearly that in a world where no one has access to a God's-eye perspective, labeling a form of speech unacceptable will always involve censoring a point of view embraced by some part of the citizenry even if it is rejected by most others. Talk of *jus cogens* cannot paper this over.

In another attempt to identify and quarantine hate speech, law professor Alon Harel divides hate speech into two kinds and argues that only one of them merits protection. Hate speech is a candidate for protection when it "is part of a broader more comprehensive and valuable form of life." Were questionable speech attached to a valuable form of life to be regulated by the state, not only would the offending expressions be condemned, but "the whole way of life of which they are a part" would be condemned too.[33] That is, if a form of life is on balance valuable, the state must put up with aspects of it—like virulent expressions of hostility to a group—that otherwise offend. So, for example, even though religions sometimes consign to hell the adherents of rival religions in words that are arguably hateful, we should, according to Harel's formula, protect those words because they issue from a life project that does more good than bad.

The word that gives Harel's game away is "valuable" ("comprehensive and valuable form of life"). It tells us that before the distinction between good (or at least less bad) hate speech and intolerable hate speech can be formulated, a prior distinction must be made between valuable and nonvaluable forms of life, and that distinction cannot be grounded in any principle. We see this when Harel specifies the features a form of life must have if it is to be placed on the right side of his dividing line: a tradition may be given the benefit of the doubt when it "includes prominent humanistic components. Islam, Judaism, and Christianity fall into such a category. Nazism and the Ku Klux Klan do not. They are hatred based traditions and, consequently, the argument is inapplicable to them."

Surely this is nothing but name-calling, a quick and dirty move designed to mask the absence of analysis by naming two groups no one would think to defend; after all, who's going to speak up for Nazis and Ku Klux Klanners? Not I, but I will point out that these groups do not consider themselves based in hatred; on the contrary, they typically claim that their actions issue from the highest ideals. On August 15, 1920, Adolf Hitler, a white supremacist if there ever was one, gave a speech entitled "Why We Are Antisemites." He began by acknowledging that many consider him and his followers "monsters," but, he insisted, we are moral men and women who hold to and preach three basic values: "work as a duty," "the necessity of bodily health and therefore also of mental health," and "a deep spiritual life," all three of which stand, he said, in contrast to the values and practices of Jews, who are always calculating profit even when they are at the opera. Now we could of course dispute the claim that Hitler and his followers are true to these values, and we could also dispute his account of how these values are fostered by Aryans and undermined by Jews, but once we did that, once we engaged his arguments rather than dismissing them out of hand, once we took the trouble to think about where he was "coming from," we would be a far cry from simply assuming that Hitler and his twenty-first-century successors operate from hatred and nothing else. Instead we would be acknowledging that their words and actions issue from a "comprehensive way of life," although it might be a form of life we do not like. "Valuable" turns out to be the compliment Harel bestows on comprehensive views he favors. It's hard to see his scheme, well-meaning though it may be, as anything more than a lineup of the groups and ideologies he and his friends despise against the groups and ideologies they approve. I happen to approve them too. But this is to say no more than that Harel's politics dovetail with mine, and therefore what he finds hateful I find hateful. That convergence, however, can hardly be cited as an *independent* justification of the line we might both draw. Robert Post has it right when he says that those "who advocate for the enforcement of fundamentals are . . . attempting to discredit and exclude those who precisely disagree with their view of fundamental values."[34] When you encounter speech that strikes you as inimical to everything you believe and cherish, you will say, "That's just awful, that's hate speech." Of course, that's not a formal definition; it is a statement of why a formal definition—general and tied to no one's parochial values— will never be achieved.

Free-speech theorist Eric Heinze is less interested in defining hate speech than he is in explaining that, however it is defined or whatever its effects, regulating it by law is destructive of the democratic process: "Viewpoint-selective penalties upon expression which is public . . . serve only to de-democratize the state."[35] Democracy, says Heinze, is "an ongoing process of public discourse," and its legitimacy is compromised if some citizens are prevented from participating because their views have been exiled. This is called the "democratic legitimacy" argument: you can't ask those who have been excluded from the public conversation to accept its outcomes.

But then, in a turn that is somewhat unexpected, Heinze relaxes the severity of his position and makes a distinction between what he calls LSPDs—"longstanding, stable and prosperous democracies" characterized by traditions that serve as "a buffer to intolerance"—and weaker democracies or nondemocracies where intolerance meets little resistance and may threaten institutions that are young and fragile. "Societies like Israel, India or Northern Ireland illustrate democratic areas in which stronger arguments can be made for hate speech bans, precisely because of their lack of a sufficiently and simultaneously longstanding, stable and prosperous character."[36] In such areas, hate-speech bans may well be a "necessary evil."

Heinze, the opponent of regulation, turns out to be not so different from Harel, the would-be engineer of regulation. Rather than dividing life projects into two kinds (those that are comprehensive in a healthy way and those that are hatred-based), Heinze divides countries into two kinds, those that need curbs on hate speech and those well developed enough to permit hate speech without placing democratic institutions in peril. And just as Harel can back up his distinction only with a political judgment as to which groups are more than hate-based, so Heinze can back up *his* distinction only with a political judgment as to which democracies are stable enough to meet his test. (I suspect that the Israelis, the Irish, and the Indians might protest his assessment of their societies.) Heinze manages to have it both ways: he can maintain his antiregulation principles at home and relax them to the point of abandoning them when he's abroad. It's a new, or perhaps not so new, form of colonialist paternalism (*Someday they will be as stable as we are and will no longer need a regulatory crutch*) that allows Heinze to argue for a public sphere where no viewpoint is proscribed (he calls his position "viewpoint absolutism") and at the same time give a reluctant okay to regulation when it occurs in countries not as advanced as ours. As a political resolution of the hate-speech dilemma, that's not bad: give up on the intractable definitional and theoretical questions and parcel out the alterna-

tives (to regulate or not regulate) to different geographical loca-
tions depending on the strength and weakness of local institutions.

For the most part, however, theorists do not give up on theory. How could they? That's what they do. They keep searching
for a formula that will allow them to avoid the conclusion that
the history of hate-speech regulation reflects nothing more noble
than the give-and-take of political contest and cannot be rendered
philosophically coherent. One way of resisting that conclusion is
to invoke the distinction between representation and the thing
represented: the activity speech describes is one thing, its representation another; you can regulate the first, but not the second. But
this is precisely the distinction MacKinnon challenges when she
insists that rather than being the *representation* of violence against
women, pornography *is* violence against women, who are directly
harmed by speech that characterizes them as sexual objects just beg-
ging for it even when they say no. Once again, MacKinnon-style
arguments undermine the speech/action distinction altogether;
everything becomes action, and the rationale for affording speech
special protection disappears. First Amendment jurisprudence, as
I noted earlier, can't allow that to happen without undoing itself;
the speech/action distinction, even if it is malleable and manipulable, must be retained. But the price of retaining it—of insisting
on speech as a distinct category—is an inability to segregate hate
speech from speech in general; either forgo the designation "hate
speech" and treat verbal assaults as the actions they are, or retain
the "hate speech" designation and be incapable of marking off the
hateful from the benign; for given that every form of speech is
hateful to someone, the category of hate speech includes, at least
potentially, everything that anyone has ever said, and one cannot
even begin to think about how and whether to regulate it. We
again arrive at the paradox I have announced several times: only if
hate speech is regarded as an action is there a coherent basis for reg-

ulating it—it produces intolerable harms—but if you regulate it on that basis, it is no longer speech. Hate speech can be addressed only when the word "speech" is deleted from the phrase and you are left with hateful *acts* the state has every right to regulate.

Who Is to Judge? The Marketplace of Ideas Once Again

Those who want to save the category of hate speech by coming up with a principled definition of it are motivated in part by fear, the fear that without an independent principle the job of deciding which forms of speech are extreme and dangerous will fall to legislators and judges—fallible human beings who form opinions on the basis of inadequate evidence and become unduly attached to those opinions once they are formed. None of us, it is said, can be trusted to be wise enough to make impartial judgments about what forms of speech should and should not be permitted. Better to leave it to the Marketplace of Ideas, to the give-and-take of rational debate engaged in by an active citizenry.

This line of reasoning is supported by two quotations from the writings of Justice Brandeis: "Sunlight is said to be the best of disinfectants" and "The remedy for bad speech is more speech, not enforced silence."[37] Together these two statements declare a faith that in time the process of democratic deliberation will generate judgments less biased and more objective than any made by a legislature or a court. Let bad ideas into the light of day and everyone will see them for what they are. Let bad ideas compete in the marketplace, where they will be defeated by better ones. (As we shall see in chapter 5, this is the argument for an unregulated internet; an internet free of monitoring is the latest version of the Marketplace of Ideas.) *The only counterargument to this optimistic picture is all of recorded history*, for what history shows is that when dangerous ideas are given a public airing, they do not wither but grow stronger. If we allow the dissemination of Holocaust denial (as the United States does and many other Western democracies don't), the result will be that more people who had never heard of it will be drawn to it. The likelihood of that happening is even greater now that the internet has given us a mode of communication at once incredibly rapid and well-nigh universal. The question may no longer be whether it is better to curb hate speech or let it into the atmosphere; that choice may be gone.

There is an even more basic problem with leaving everything to the Marketplace of Ideas. If we need the marketplace because as beings too much in love with our own views we cannot be trusted to make good judgments, won't that same fallibility (no more removable than original sin; it *is* original sin) prevent us from being able to determine when the marketplace has finally done its work and we can rest securely in what it has delivered? If no government or court can be trusted to make the necessary distinctions, neither can the marketplace be trusted to do the job, for its revolutions mark nothing more than the temporary ascendancy of someone's or some group's point of view. And if there is no way of knowing for sure if and when the marketplace has produced outcomes we can safely embrace, isn't it just a device for delaying decisions when making a decision may well be what the situation requires? Could the Marketplace of Ideas be nothing more than a convenient cover for the reluctance of institutions like courts and legislatures to do the job assigned them? Is the Marketplace of Ideas the free-speech offshoot of capitalism (as the very phrase suggests), asking us to be confident in its benign workings even though much of the evidence is to the contrary? Is it really true that the more information we have, no matter what its source or the intentions of those who produce it, the better able we will be to sort out the true from the false? Either we take our fallibility seriously and acknowledge that no amount of time will eliminate it, in which case we might as well act on what we know *now* (though every act will be a risk), or we make love to our fallibility—make it into a principle of inaction—and allow it to tie our hands at the very moment that damage, verbal and otherwise, is being done. It may be, as the legal scholar Brian Leiter says, that "it is long past time to abandon the implausible idea that 'free speech' . . . is an obvious force for further enlightenment and human well-being."[38]

It is an impatience with the marketplace's slow, very slow, rectification of injustice that helps explain the hostility toward the First Amendment displayed by today's campus protestors. They argue that by affording free speech to people spreading vicious and harmful ideas—ideas like Holocaust denial and racial inferiority— that have been labeled baseless by credentialed experts, we give renewed life to what might otherwise remain dead and buried. In many ways campuses are the location of a continuing seminar on the questions and issues we have been surveying in this chapter, and it is to that seminar that we now turn.

CHAPTER 3

Why Freedom of Speech Is Not an Academic Value

Freedom of Speech versus Freedom of Inquiry: Universities Are Not in the Democracy Business

In early March 2019, President Trump announced in a speech that he would soon sign an executive order "requiring colleges and universities to support free speech if they want federal research funds." In response, Terry Hartle, a senior vice president of the American Council of Education, insisted that on American campuses "free speech is a core value."[1] By replying in that way, Hartle confirmed the assumption implicit in Trump's announcement: freedom of speech is essential to the activities of research and teaching, and a college or university that fails to protect it is compromising its mission. Trump is saying that colleges and universities are not living up to their free-speech obligations. Hartle is saying that they are. I am saying that the concern Trump and Hartle share is misplaced: for the most part colleges and universities don't have free-speech obligations because freedom of speech is not an academic value.

I know that this assertion will strike many as tendentious and just plain wrong. Here is a recent statement (2015) by a faculty committee at the University of Chicago: "From its very founding, the University of Chicago has dedicated itself to the preservation and celebration of the freedom of expression as an essential element of the University's culture."[2] In *Speaking Freely: Why Universities Must Defend Free Speech*, Keith Whittington echoes this First Amendment party line when he declares, "[A] robust commitment to free speech on campus is essential."[3] My challenge to that popular view (the Chicago statement has been endorsed by a number of other universities) depends on a distinction between freedom of speech and freedom of inquiry. Freedom of speech is a democratic value. It says that in a democracy government should neither anoint nor stigmatize particular forms of speech but act as an honest broker providing a framework and a forum for the competition of ideas and policies. In this vision, every voice has a right to be heard, at least theoretically. (In fact, differences in resources will almost always translate into differences in the size of the audience one can reach.) In the academy, on the other hand, free inquiry, not free speech, is the reigning ethic, and academic inquiry is engaged in only by those who have been certified as competent; not every voice gets to be heard. The right to speak in the scholarly conversation does not come with membership; it is granted only to those who have survived a series of vettings and are left standing after countless others have been sent out of the room. Determining who will *not* be allowed to speak is the regular business of departments, search committees, promotion committees, deans, provosts, presidents, and editors of learned journals. Speech in the academy is scripted and limited to concerns and perspectives that are recognized by the profession as distinctively academic. Students and professors who cry "Free speech!" at the drop of a hat are invoking a value that is more often than not beside the academic point. Whittington has it exactly wrong when he says that "the truth-seeking mission of universities dovetails with the truth-seeking values of free speech."

Let me illustrate with a few examples. Is the instructor who cuts off a student in mid-sentence and says "That's not an argument we'll be pursuing here" violating the student's free-speech rights? Is the department that mandates a particular set of texts in a core course and disallows departures from the official list violating the academic freedom rights of an instructor who would prefer another list or no list at all? Is a department that rejects a faculty member's proposal for a course on the grounds that it doesn't fit in with the department's priorities stifling that faculty member's freedom of expression? Is a department that refuses to hire or promote a candidate because his or her publications were judged "below our standards" silencing that candidate in a way that presents a First Amendment issue? All of these examples are obviously absurd, for singly and together they amount to a misunderstanding of what goes on in a college or a university: not the proliferation of voices by some democratic principle but the exercise of judgment by persons and bodies authorized to decide which voices are worthy of being heard and which are not. Students are not authorized to exercise that judgment; they are apprentices, and they have no right to a voice in the content or structure of their education. (An instructor may choose to give them a voice, but that would be a voluntary act, not a required one.) Departments, not faculty members, determine which materials are properly taught in which courses, and to the extent that faculty members are free to choose their own materials, that freedom has been granted to them; it is not theirs by right. Candidates for hiring and promotion do not get to name the standards by which they will be evaluated. Academic inquiry, then, is not free in the First Amendment sense; it is free only in a very special sense: the path of inquiry is open and should not be blocked either by putting the stamp of approval on particular points of view in advance or by dismissing other points of view before they are heard and evaluated. Nor should inquiry be distorted by external pressures, whether they stem from churches, politicians, parents, donors, or corporate interests. The freedom valued in the academy is the freedom (also a constraint in the form of an obligation) to follow the evidence wherever it leads, and that freedom carries with it the responsibility to determine which evidence should be retained and which discarded, which speakers should be attended to and which sent away. Obviously, there is nothing democratic about the course of this inquiry; it would be better described as Darwinian, the survival if not of the fittest then of those who still have a place at the table after all the votes have been taken.

What I've just said applies to both private and public universities, even though only the latter are subject to legal penalties for violating the First Amendment. It is true, of course, that private universities need not respect First Amendment obligations (they have the same discretionary latitude as any other private association or business), but nevertheless most do.[4] To be sure, there are differences. A private university affiliated with a religious establishment may require that its senior administrators be congregants, while a public university could not announce the same criterion without falling afoul of the Establishment Clause. But in most other respects, private and public universities adhere to the same principles—not the principles of the First Amendment (which, I am arguing, have less relevance to higher education than is often assumed) but the principles of the academic enterprise, which include first and foremost the principle of pursuing inquiry in the absence of any pre-decision about the worthiness or unworthiness of particular ideas. Religiously affiliated institutions have long been under suspicion because they are thought to violate this principle. Their very status as educational institutions has been questioned because, as the authors of the American Association of University Professors statement on academic freedom put it in 1915, "they do not, at least as regards one particular subject, accept the principles of freedom and inquiry."[5] The presumption is that a sectarian school would not hire an instructor who held the faith in contempt or believed and preached that God does not exist. But even if this were so with respect to a particular institution, a huge percentage of what its instructors would be teaching would look just like what was being taught at the University of Michigan or Williams College. I have been a faculty member at both public and private universities, including two that are avowedly sectarian, and I can honestly say that the feel of the enterprise I was participating in did not vary with the public, private, or sectarian designation. Every day I was on the job (including days when I was sitting in a faculty meeting), I felt that I was just being an academic, and my understanding of what that involved was always the same. Both private universities like Yale, Harvard, and Princeton (which did not abolish compulsory chapel attendance until 1962) and major sectarian universities like Notre Dame, Holy Cross, Catholic University, Georgetown, Yeshiva, and Brigham Young consider themselves bound by the protocols periodically announced by the AAUP. Those protocols—which are cultural, not legal—occasionally intersect with, but are not equivalent to, First Amendment protocols. They are *professional*, not constitutional, protocols, and it is within their assumptions and demands that my analysis is mounted. That is why the distinction between private and public does not register strongly in these pages.

So I say again that freedom of speech is not an academic value, whether or not the college or university is public or private. Accuracy of speech is an academic value. (You should check your facts and identify your sources.) Completeness of speech is an academic value. (You should not leave out evidence that counts against your case.) Relevance of speech is an academic value. (You should not go off on tangents either in the classroom or in your scholarship.) Each of these values is directly related to academic inquiry, to the goal of arriving at the truth of some disputed matter in the humanities, social sciences, or physical sciences. Freedom of speech stands in an oblique relationship to that goal, sometimes to the academic point but most of the time not.

Free Speech and Extracurricular Contexts

Of course today many of the debates about free speech occur not in the context of classroom activities but in the arena of extracurricular activities. "Extra" means outside, not at the center of. Activities that fall under that rubric are not essential to the university's mission and can be dispensed with. A college or university that just had students, faculty, a library, laboratories, and a computing center would be a university even if there were no student union, no food court, no athletic events, no rock concerts, no auditorium for visiting speakers, no bowling alley, no gymnasium with a swimming pool, no climbing walls. If, however, the things I have just listed were present in a space, but students, faculty members, and libraries were not, what you would have is not a university or college but a playground or a theme park. So colleges and universities are not under an obligation to include all these extras, although political and economic realities today pretty much dictate that they must have some of these facilities and events if they wish to attract a sufficient number of students.

Here's where the trouble begins. How does a university administration determine which events shall be authorized and which events shall be turned away? And if an event has been authorized by the proper procedures, how, then, does the administration deal with the possibility of disruption and even violence? These questions, which are being asked by every administration, sound as if they were deep, that is, related to significant moral and philosophical issues. They are not. They are largely questions of management and crowd control. Remember, the university is not presiding over these occasions in the same way it presides over its classrooms and laboratories. The university is merely allowing a space it owns to be used for extracurricular purposes. The university may believe that these uses enhance the undergraduate experience or provide perspectives students should be introduced to, but that will be so only in a few cases. Rock band concerts and visiting provocateurs are in the entertainment, not the education, business. In fact, all extracurricular activities fall into the category of entertainment, and once that is understood, the obligation of the administration comes into focus: invite those who are in fact likely to entertain, including entertaining in the mode of provocation, but take care that the entertainment doesn't get out of hand and lead to the possible destruction of the facility that will welcome another form of entertainment next week. What you want is an experience that is stimulating, but not too stimulating; voices and fists may be raised but no blows landed. No one should be bored and everyone should leave thinking "I had a fine time."

I play in a regular basketball game with other old codgers, and after each game one of my fellow septuagenarians says the same thing: "It was a good workout and no one was hurt." (Not said on the day I broke my hand in January 2018.) That should be the benediction uttered after every campus event. The problem is that in the current campus atmosphere, assuring that happy outcome can cost a fortune. The University of California, Berkeley, spent over six hundred thousand dollars in efforts to keep the peace during a lecture given by a controversial speaker. Is a university required to risk bankruptcy in order to avoid being found guilty of viewpoint discrimination against some visiting speakers? It was to answer that question that Berkeley's chancellor established a university commission charged with fashioning policies that would both honor everyone's free-speech rights and maintain the order and security of university events. The commission reported in 2018 and made a number of recommendations, including requiring student organizations to provide volunteers at "potentially disruptive events" and submit a statement explaining the educational rationale for any such event.[6] It remains a question as to whether these requirements are consistent with the First Amendment since they would likely curb the speech activities of some groups and not of others.

Robert Post, former dean of the Yale Law School, would say that is the wrong question; the right one is *Does this event or speaker contribute to the university's missions of research and education?* This means, he explains, that speakers should be invited "*because* they serve these missions,"[7] and when they do not, failing to invite them or revoking an invitation too hastily tendered should raise no First Amendment issues because educational, not First Amendment, values are paramount. Post neatly sidesteps the charge of viewpoint discrimination because what he is discriminating against is not a point of view as such, but a point of view that does not mesh with the purposes of the institution. "Nonmeshing" is a judgment that might be applied to speech on any side of the political/cultural divide; the point is not what the speech at issue says but whether what it says is helpful to the educational process.

In Post's account, the university is a unitary thing: it is not divided into curricular and extracurricular sectors. He rejects the division of the campus into two zones, as proposed by UC Berkeley's Law School dean Erwin Chemerinsky and UC Irvine Chancellor Howard Gillman: "*a professional zone* which . . . imposes an obligation of responsible discourse and responsible conduct in formal educational and scholarly settings" and "a larger *free speech zone* which exists outside scholarly and administrative settings and where the only restrictions are those of society at large."[8] Post is saying that there is only a single zone and that in a space owned and policed by the university nothing exists outside the educational setting and its purposes. Therefore nothing should escape the monitoring of administrators: "[T]he *entire* purpose of a university is to educate and to expand knowledge, and so everything a university does must be justified by reference to these twin purposes."[9] Post's position is more radical than mine. He eliminates the category of entertainment and the special obligation of administrators to acquire crowd-control skills, and substitutes the general requirement of conformity with the educational mission. He extends my argument that free-speech values do not rule the classroom to extracurricular contexts, which in his account are no longer extracurricular because they are an extension of the principles informing the classroom. Administrators needn't tie themselves in knots over First Amendment issues; they should just remember the mission of the institution they preside over and say yes and no to speakers on that basis, without any free-speech anxiety. (Richard Spencer, no; Charles Murray, yes; David Duke, no; Betsy DeVos, absolutely; Donald Trump, of course.)

Dean Chemerinsky disagrees strongly. He resists the distinction between freedom of inquiry and freedom of speech, the distinction Post succinctly articulates when he says that "First Amendment rights were developed and defined in order to protect the political life of the nation, but life within universities is not a mirror of that life." Yes it is, Chemerinsky replies. In his view, there is no distance at all between free-speech priorities and academic priorities: "The assumption of freedom of speech and of academic freedom is that education is enhanced when there is more speech."[10] No, Post and

I would say; education is enhanced when care is taken that the speech produced in academic contexts is a contribution to the academic enterprise. The proposition that speech, no matter what its content or effects, is per se a contribution to that enterprise subordinates academic concerns to the political concern of including as many voices as possible and by doing so denies the university a life of its own shaped and informed by its own protocols. The irony is that arguments like Chemerinsky's, when deployed by administrators (and he of course is one himself), allow them to abdicate their responsibilities and give them over to a piece of the Constitution that has nothing to do with the enterprise in their care. As Post says, they are "blinded by a mechanical doctrine that has no relevance to the phenomena it is supposed to control." University administrators who spend their time worrying about whose First Amendment rights may have been violated have taken their eyes off the job they were hired to perform.

So administrators facing threats of disruption and violence can do one of three things: (1) don't have any extracurricular events; (2) if you choose to have them, come up with a crowd-control plan and the resources to implement it; or (3) invoke Post's test question—Does the event further the university's mission?—and just say no when the answer is no. The one thing they shouldn't do is hide behind the First Amendment.

What Do Students Want?

If administrators more than occasionally invoke free-speech doctrine as an excuse for avoiding their responsibilities—"Sorry, there's nothing I can do; it's the First Amendment"—today's militant students scorn free-speech doctrine because it's an obstacle to their doing whatever they like when a speaker whose views they oppose comes to town. Of course not all students are militant; most of today's students keep their heads down and focus on the requirements for the degree they hope will lead to employment. So in the remarks that follow, I'm thinking mainly of activist students (situated largely on the left) who lobby for a role in the formation of the curriculum and in the choice of texts to be included in the syllabus of a particular course. In places like Oberlin and Amherst, students have made their wishes known by presenting a list of demands, as long as eighteen pages, to the administration, including the demands that only speakers they approve of should be invited to campus and only faculty they approve of should be hired and retained. These students, often a minority, but a minority with a loud voice, tend to be wholly persuaded of the rightness of their views; they don't see why they should be forced to listen to, or even be in the presence of, views they know to be false. They wish to institute what I would call a "virtue regime," where people who say the right kind of thing get to speak or teach and those who are on the wrong side of history (as they see it) don't. And since they regard themselves as bearers of truth rather than as advocates—they're not making an argument; they're just standing up for what is obviously right—they feel justified in opposing the bearers of falsehood by every means available, even if that involves shouting them down, pelting them with eggs, and putting them in the hospital, something that happened to a faculty member at Middlebury College. [11]

Whether knowingly or not, the activist students are echoing the words of Herbert Marcuse in his classic essay *Repressive Tolerance*.[12] Marcuse rejects the liberal practice of allowing all ideas to enter the mix in the hope that the marketplace will sort the good from the bad. This, he explains, amounts to a one-size-fits-all tolerance, which, because it is extended to every idea, legitimates as plausible alternatives "policies, conditions, and modes of behavior which should not be tolerated because they are impeding, if not destroying, the chances of creating an existence without fear and misery." Therefore, the realization of true tolerance requires "intolerance toward prevailing policies, attitudes, opinions."

In a postscript, Marcuse acknowledges that his goal was to shift "the balance between Right and Left by restraining the liberty of the Right." This is justified, he believes, because right-wing ideas are plainly wrong and have no right to be heard. Marcuse scoffs at the objection that "such a policy would do away with the sacred liberal principle of equality 'for the other side.'" "I maintain," he declares, "that there are issues where either there is no 'other side' . . . or where 'the other side' is demonstrably regressive and impedes possible improvement of the human condition." Improving the human condition is a priority to which the abstract priority of hearing all voices must be subordinated. Now, one can understand this as a political strategy, but its spirit—*Let's win the battle by any means available*—is antithetical to the academic enterprise where giving "the other side" a hearing is exactly what goes on, or should go on, in the classroom: you should consider all the arguments in the field, even those with which you at least initially disagree, and proceed to assess them by the tried-and-true standards of deliberative inquiry. Students impelled by a sense of their own virtue and by the obvious (to them) correctness of their own views aren't going to do that. Instead they are going to do what Marcuse urges: shut down the conversation, secure in the conviction that by doing so they advance the causes of justice and equality.

Mark Bray, a theorist of the Antifa (antifascist) movement, provides a Marcuse-like justification of student protest behavior. Bray rejects the "classical liberal notion" that "sees the role of government as that of referee in a game that all political tendencies are invited to play." Regarding alt-right propaganda as speech or opinion "which is just as legitimate as any other" doesn't "take seriously the ramifications that such views can and do have in the world around us."[13] More direct action is required, actions that deny "fascists a platform" for their views and "make it politically, socially, economically, and sometime physically costly to articulate them." Bray notes the objection that these tactics "make us no better than Nazis," but he replies by declaring the superiority of the ethical sentiments he and his colleagues are moved by: "We must point out that our critique is not against violence, incivility, discrimination or disrupting speeches in the abstract, but against those who do so in the service of white supremacy, hetero-patriarchy, class oppression and genocide." *Suppression by the Nazis was wrong because the ideas they suppressed were good; suppression by us is right because what we suppress is bad.* As a theory of political action, Bray's argument—*Let's not cling to some formal principle of the equality of all ideas while some ideas continue to do bad work*—has some appeal, but as a recipe for campus behavior, it must be rejected for the same reason Marcuse's argument must be rejected: it contravenes the spirit of the educational enterprise. If you want to advance the ideas and policies you believe in and not give the other fellow the time of day, get out of the academy. Keith Whittington, whose commentary is quite good when he's not retailing free-speech pieties, nails it: "A campus that seeks to plug its ears against the possibility of hearing 'controversial statements' has abandoned the scholarly enterprise."[14]

The scholarly enterprise has also been abandoned whenever students and/or administrators discipline or sanction a faculty member who has taken extra-academic stances they don't like. In early 2019, there were demands that Harvard residential faculty dean Ronald Sullivan Jr. be removed from his position because he had joined the legal team defending Harvey Weinstein. Sullivan's critics asked how he could at once be part of Weinstein's defense and carry out his obligation to provide a safe environment for students in his role as faculty dean. The answer is that the two contexts of action—taking on a client and monitoring the safety of a residential college—have nothing to do with one another. On the one hand, Sullivan is performing in the best tradition of our justice system when he agrees to defend—legally, not personally; this is a crucial distinction—an unpopular public figure; on the other hand, he is being faithful to the responsibilities he assumed when he stepped into the role of faculty dean. In both contexts he should be judged by the protocols and principles of the practice he is engaged in: in one case the practice of providing citizens, no matter how notorious they may be, with a defense; and in the other case, ensuring that students at Harvard will be afforded the dignity and feeling of well-being they deserve. Performing responsibly in either practice requires that you not bring it before the bar of the other. You can't be a good defense attorney if you're wondering what your students will think, and you can't be a good steward of student life if your chief concern is for the predators who might threaten its serenity. Some student protesters carried signs saying "Do your job." Sullivan *was* doing his job, which is not to harmonize all aspects of his behavior under one ideal measure but to conform his behavior to the principles of the enterprise in which he is at the moment situated.[15]

Today's student protestors join a long line of persons and constituencies bent on making the groves of academe bear alien fruit. The difference—and it is all to the students' credit—is that while founders, churchmen, donors, politicians, and corporations typically seek power in order to make universities instruments of their parochial interests, student protestors seek to advance the perfection of the world. The idea—and it is a thrilling one—is that if we can identify and remedy the injustices that configure campus life, we can set the world a virtuous example that will in time redeem the mortal condition. I do not quarrel with the ideal. I quarrel only with the assumption that it is the university's job to implement it. If universities allow their energies and resources to be put in the service of tasks other than the task assigned to them—improving the state of knowledge—they risk losing their distinctiveness and with it the rationale for their very existence. The goal of university activity is not perfection of the human condition but the maintenance of a way of life—the life of disinterested contemplation—which, because it will not survive on its own (too many forces are arrayed against it), requires vigilance and a concerted effort to prevent its being subordinated to something else. Knowingly or not, the more militant of the student protestors do not join in that effort, but subvert it.

The Rhetoric of Virtue: How Students Persuade Themselves That They Are Doing the Right Thing

The protestors support their actions with the recitation and invocation of a handful of now familiar words and phrases: "trigger warnings," "micro-aggressions," "safe spaces," "nonplatforming," "cultural appropriation." I am by no means the first to point out that the actions called for by these slogans undermine the purpose of higher education: the concern for the advancement of knowledge is replaced with a concern for the emotional equilibrium of students who are to be protected from ideas they might find distressing. What is it that students wish to be safe from? Ideas and viewpoints that run counter to what they already believe. In short, they don't want to learn anything. What is a trigger warning? A warning by an instructor to students that they might be distressed by what they are about to hear or read and therefore should have the right to avoid the distress by not reading or not listening. In short, they don't want to learn anything. What are micro-aggressions? Mistakes, almost all of them unavoidable (unless you're an intellectual colossus who bestrides every territory in the vast cultural world), made by those who speak from inside a culture to others who inhabit a culture the micro-aggressor does not know.[16] Calling out micro-aggressions amounts to a game of "Gotcha!" There will always be something an instructor says that offends someone, and according to the logic of micro-aggressions, he or she deserves to be condemned for saying it. The only way to steer clear of micro-aggressions is to say nothing or to say only things preapproved by the virtue-monitors, who again don't want to learn anything. And as for cultural appropriation, the idea that a culture owns a form of music or a mode of dress or a style of cooking is racism pure and simple; it makes sense only if those modes and styles have their source in blood, if playing certain chords or preparing certain foods is a skill that has been inherited. Arguing that African Americans have unique title to jazz or rap or cornrows is no different from arguing that African Americans lack the intelligence to be first-rate analytical philosophers. Indeed they are the same argument, for each identifies a capacity or an incapacity with a racial identity. If, however, the ability to perform or create in particular ways has its source in culture, then anyone who takes the time to be initiated into that culture has as much right to the clothing or music or food as anyone else. Of course there is another form of cultural appropriation whose consequences are economic: the phenomenon of mainstream artists plundering the work of minority musicians without either due acknowledgment or compensation is well known and the just basis of complaint. That's not what today's students are complaining about, however; they are making a general point about what belongs to a race as a matter of racial right. In effect, the ban on cultural appropriation is a ban on entering and taking possession of hitherto unfamiliar contexts of experience.[17] And again, those who have imposed the ban or accept its imposition don't want to learn anything.

In a widely circulated and influential essay (now a book), Greg

Lukianoff and Jonathan Haidt also reject the discourse of trigger warnings, micro-aggressions, and safe spaces, but what worries them is the relationship between these concepts and the moral and emotional health of students. Their complaint is that policies protecting students from unsettling texts and discussions contribute to a fragility that "prepares them poorly for professional life, which often demands intellectual engagement with people and ideas one might find uncongenial."[18] As an antidote Lukianoff and Haidt offer the techniques of cognitive-behavioral therapy, which, they say, are designed to mitigate if not entirely negate habits of mind that lead to the kind of "bad thinking" students currently exhibit. If students were taught early on to practice cognitive-behavioral therapy, they could participate in the strengthening of their own psyches and become less vulnerable to the fears that render them unwilling to hear points of view they find disagreeable. "You can master your desires and thoughts," the authors promise. Maybe yes, maybe no (for the record, I think no), but whatever its strengths or weaknesses, the Lukianoff-Haidt analysis is off to the side of what I take to be the key question, which is not the relationship of trigger warnings and safe spaces to student emotional health but the relationship of trigger warnings and safe spaces to the university's core activity of exploring issues in an effort to determine the truth of a matter. Surely that activity is undermined by decisions to disallow certain arguments before they are fully considered because they might cause discomfort.

In the end, Lukianoff and Haidt have more in common with the students they criticize than they think, for they share with them a concern to foster mental and emotional resilience; it's just that they have different notions as to how it might be achieved. It's the difference between tough love and protective love. But neither side of that argument is on point, for it can't be the purpose of college and university life either to toughen up student sensibilities or to be solicitous of them. It's the purpose of college and university life to draw students into an ongoing conversation presided over by academic, not psychological, protocols. Student sensibilities will, no doubt, be what they are, and they will above all be variable. Pedagogy, if it really is pedagogy and not therapy, cannot be centered on them. (Of course this doesn't mean that an instructor should be dismissive or abusive; common courtesy should be the background norm in any classroom.)

Meanwhile the virtue mantras continue to be invoked and they continue to do work, and that work is generally bad. Witness what happened at Reed College when a group called Reedies against Racism (RAR) interrupted and shut down sections of the college's signature humanities course, Hum 110. Although the course contained materials from the ancient Mediterranean, Mesopotamia, Persia, and Egypt, the protesting students found it "Eurocentric," "Caucasoid," and therefore "oppressive." The very fact of the course was found traumatizing by some of those who objected to it. Protestors arrived in classrooms brandishing signs and photographs of African Americans slain by police. Some instructors were more than intimidated; they were themselves traumatized and unable to continue. The Reed administration gave in to a number of the student demands and set up a series of meetings between protestors and professors. The meetings were discontinued when some of the RAR members complained of being "forced to sit in hours of fruitless meetings listening to full-grown adults cry about Aristotle."[19] The more the administration responded to the protests, the more destructive the protestors became. No one should be surprised. Once the admittedly artificial but crucial separation of the academic world from the world of politics is relaxed, there is no stopping place. Either the norms underwriting the conversation are rigorously academic and are maintained as such, or the category of the academic disappears.

It is misleading to call controversies like the one at Reed free-speech controversies. The issue is much deeper: Can an enterprise dedicated to the disinterested contemplation of ideas, no matter what their source or provenance, survive a demand that before an idea is let into the classroom, it must pass a political litmus test? This question would seem to supply its own answer: no. Any other answer is imaginable only if the purpose of the enterprise is discarded and replaced by a frankly political agenda whose point is not to study ideas but to promote those ideas that support the students' (and some faculty members') ideological point of view and to exclude those ideas that don't. That agenda prevailed at Reed, and its triumph had nothing to do with either the promotion or the limiting of free speech. It was a political putsch plain and simple, even if free-speech rhetoric was deployed on all sides.

No reader of the previous paragraphs will be in doubt as to my sympathies. But Ulrich Baer, a professor and administrator at New York University, offers a more generous account of the student protesters and the concerns informing their words and actions. In a *New York Times* op-ed and later in a book-length statement, Baer argues that what the students are so worked up about is the spectacle of administrators smugly invoking the First Amendment as a rationale for inviting to campus speakers whose assertion of racial and gender hierarchies, with straight white males always at the top, is an implicit and sometimes explicit undermining of the right of members of the audience to be there, or to be anywhere. These students, he says, are being told that they are not equal, and equality, Baer insists, rather than an arid and knee-jerk First Amendment absolutism, is the value we should be standing up for. "A campus visitor who argues that some students are inherently inferior materially undermines the conditions that make speech free."[20] The students, he continues, wonder why universities that regularly exclude from the classroom discarded and disproven ideas about science and medicine offer a platform for the rehearsal of discarded and disproven ideas about race and gender and then expect members of the demeaned groups to embrace the occasion as an affirmation of free speech. I suspect that Baer's articulation of the students' position is more nuanced than anything they themselves typically offer; nevertheless he does have a point, although in my mind, it is not one that excuses the actions taken by the protestors at Reed. Any disagreement between us, however, is perhaps smaller than the view we share: that campus speech controversies are not really about free speech but about something else for which free-speech issues are the proxy—equality in Baer's view, the maintenance of the academic enterprise in mine.

So I return again to the main argument of this chapter: despite media reports to the contrary, there are very few free-speech issues on campus. Most of the issues labeled "free speech" are really issues of professional demarcations (Do students have academic freedom rights?) or issues of management (What contingency plans should administrators have in place in anticipation of unruly protests?). These matters certainly display a "free-speech element," for the production of speech is often involved, but resolutions of them do not depend on the invocation of traditional First Amendment concerns. The issues in play are professional, not moral or philosophical. Of course on some level, moral and philosophical issues are always to the point when thinking about the role and function of universities. One might ask, for example, whether higher education should be publicly supported at all; one might question the role of the university in credentialing experts and thus (according to some) participating in a conspiracy against innovation. But questions that basic have already been answered (at least provisionally) when the school doors open, and, although they could always be raised again, it is not the university's obligation to raise them daily. (A university of course could devote a symposium to such foundational questions, but the symposium would unfold against the background of the answers currently in place.) It *is* the university's obligation to manage the energies of its constituencies in a way that is minimally disruptive of the core work of academic life as it is presently understood.

Divesting from Fossil Fuels: Should Universities Speak Out?

Still, there are some campus controversies that do directly implicate First Amendment concerns, and often they involve demands by students and/or faculty that the university, in the person of its administrators, take a position on controversial issues. In recent years students and some faculty have asked universities to say no to fossil fuels by divesting themselves of fossil fuel stocks. The spirit and ideology of the movement are captured in this statement by Chloe Maxmin, a student activist at the time: "The divestment movement . . . aims to stigmatize the fossil fuel industry by rebranding it as a social pariah and a rogue political force that preys on our future. We want to make it socially unacceptable for politicians and institutions to support a reckless industry that manipulates the political system and values short term profits over humanity's survival."[21] Maxmin clearly sees that if a university were to divest, it would be positioning itself on one side of a political dispute and therefore making a political statement. No doubt, at many colleges and universities a majority of the students and faculty is on that side and believes, indeed, that there is no other side and surely no one that deserves to be heard. The students are asking universities to do what they themselves more and more tend to do: substitute for academic-style deliberation the declaration of what they take to be the undoubted truth. Why shouldn't a university line up with the angels?

Those against divestment will argue not that the truth is on the other side but that this is the kind of truth on which universities shouldn't pronounce. They will say that the truth universities are committed to establishing is the truth about factual matters in the humanities, social sciences, and physical sciences. Do migration patterns in the Southwest suggest an emerging Democratic Party majority? Is chronic fatigue syndrome a virus or a deficiency of the immune system? Those who debate questions like these will give reasons and listen to counterreasons and participate in a collaborative effort to determine, insofar as possible, what is the case. The relevant question is *What is the fact of the matter?*, not *What should we, as individuals or as a nation, do to solve a problem?* When we turn to that second question, truth is still a concern, but it is a truth about the soundness of a policy. Is it true that we should strike North Korea preemptively? Is it true that we should legalize assisted suicide? These are political and moral questions, and while there is surely a truth to be determined about them, it is not a truth a university properly seeks, although it would be entirely proper to survey in a classroom the various answers offered by researchers in the field. Just don't go the next step and take a vote and send your students out committed to a political position.

This severe point of view in which universities must have a hands-off policy and therefore a "say nothing" policy with respect to matters not strictly academic was succinctly announced by the provost of the University of Wisconsin at Madison when, in 2003, he met with students who were urging the administration to take a stand on the then impending invasion of Iraq. He said, "[T]he University of Wisconsin does not have a foreign policy." This profound witticism was recently given a more prosaic formulation by Drew Gilpin Faust, then president of Harvard, when she rejected student demands that her university divest itself of fossil fuel stocks: "We should . . . be very wary of steps intended to instrumentalize our endowment in ways that would appear to position the university as a political actor rather than an academic institution."[22] From Faust's perspective, divesting from fossil fuels would be the equivalent of the university's announcing that it was supporting a particular candidate in an election. Many faculty as well as most students would welcome such an announcement, but what Faust is saying is that the moment such an announcement is made, the institution has ceased to be academic and has become a political actor. One might argue that by investing in fossil fuels a university is taking a political position. No, it isn't, if the reason for investing is a financial and fiduciary one. Ordinarily, a university's investment in a stock does not amount to an endorsement of the activities the corporation engages in. But singling out a stock for disinvestment does amount to a disapproval of those activities and hence is a blatantly political act.

So there are at least two reasons for colleges and universities to refrain from speaking out on controversial political issues (unless of course the issue touches directly on the health and flourishing of the university; in that case the duty of the university is to insert itself into the controversy, for in doing so it would not be forsaking the academic enterprise but rising to its defense). The first reason is implicit in Faust's statement: because teaching and research are the university's distinctive activities, putting a university's resources in the service of an activity to the side of its mission will implicitly decertify it and raise questions about the rationale for its existence. If at bottom the university is a political actor with classrooms, why not dispense with the classrooms and go right to the political agenda? The other reason for universities to refrain from taking political stances is that once they do they become vulnerable to constituencies (and there will always be some) whose convictions lie on the other side of the question; they will become vulnerable also to the accusation that they are playing politics, which is of course what they would be doing, usually badly. So you can urge universities to remain silent either because you believe that the integrity of the enterprise requires that they not pronounce on political matters or because you fear the consequences of inserting universities directly into the political arena where they would likely be overmatched.

There are many who see statements like Faust's as a dereliction of duty on the part of universities and university administrators, who, after all, occupy a privileged position of influence and therefore should exert that influence in an effort to better the society in particular and the human condition in general. Those who think that way will not want the university to refrain from pronouncing on controversial matters, but instead will urge senior administrators to speak out and play a direct role in both the formation and the guidance of public conversation and debate. They will find support in the 1915 statement of the American Association of University Professors on academic freedom and tenure. The authors of that document saw it as the job of universities to produce experts who will correct the errors of popular opinion and "retrain" (their word) a democracy that may have been led astray by untutored voices.[23] In their view, the university is a social and political institution that has ambitions and obligations well beyond the classroom and the research laboratory. Needless to say, I set myself against that position. Of course it is true that universities are politically *situated*; everything about them, from their incorporation to their funding, their tax status, and the state services they rely on, is enmeshed in politics. But that is quite different from saying that those who work inside universities should conduct themselves as political *actors*. It is one thing to be embedded in a structure made possible by political activities; it is quite another to be acting as a political agent within that structure. The first is unavoidable; the second, I think, is to be avoided no matter what the temptation.

I know that my view of academic life and work is unfashion-able. The belief that universities have more general obligations to the public and to their students and should not confine themselves to honoring and maintaining what I have called academic values is held by many, on the left and on the right, and the reasons they give for that belief are often attractive and seem compelling. But I remain convinced that an uncompromisingly narrow understand-ing of what universities are is necessary to their survival and flour-ishing and will in the end garner more support than a surrender (which would have to be performed differently at different times) to the political urgencies of the day. The university that rigorously distances itself from politics will be at once true to its mission and more likely to prosper politically.

This opposition between those who think (as I do) that univer-sities should stick to their academic knitting and those whose view of the university's role is more expansive often sits in the back-ground of many campus controversies, dictating their shape even when that opposition is not specifically referenced. Different ideas about the purposes universities should serve will translate into different understandings of the actions appropriate to students, faculty, and administrators; while those different understandings will sometimes take the surface form of free-speech claims and counterclaims, the underlying debate is often less about free speech than it is about the scope and limits of academic performance on the part of various actors.

The Amy Wax Story

Consider as an example the recent fortunes or misfortunes of Amy Wax, a professor of law at the University of Pennsylvania. Wax's conflict with her colleagues and her dean was sometimes framed in free-speech terms, but it was really a disagreement about professional responsibilities.

Here's what happened. In August 2017, Wax coauthored with law professor Larry Alexander (University of San Diego) an op-ed titled "Paying the Price for a Breakdown of the Country's Bourgeois Culture." It was published in the *Philadelphia Inquirer* and was illustrated by a picture of John Wayne, either a provocation or a reassurance, depending on whether a reader was liberal or conservative. Wax and Alexander began by listing the ills of the present day: too many unqualified job applicants, too few males in the workplace, opioid addiction, violence in the inner cities, children born out of wedlock, and an undergraduate student body less skilled academically than that of two dozen other countries. They then said that while the causes of these phenomena are "multiple and complex," one primary cause in their opinion is the "breakdown of the country's bourgeois culture," the culture in which you were supposed to get married before you had children, remain married, get the education you need for gainful employment, work hard, be a patriot, be civic minded, be respectful of authority, and avoid coarse language. According to Wax and Alexander, these "basic cultural precepts" were in force from the late 1940s to the mid-1960s, and we would be better off if they were revived today.[24]

Now it is easy to mount a criticism of this argument or to declare, as one prominent legal academic (Brian Leiter) has, that it is "silly."[25] One can also imagine colleagues of Wax's and Alexander's in their respective law schools strongly disagreeing with their analysis and pointing out, as some did, that behind the façade of the 1950s were swept-under-the-rug evils like racism, anti-Semitism, violence against women, and unapologetic homophobia. Still, however wise or foolish they may have been, Wax and Alexander had every right to offer their analysis of the culture's ills in a public forum, and their colleagues also had every right to criticize that analysis in the halls of the law school or in print. But when thirty-three of Wax's colleagues wrote an open letter to the University of Pennsylvania community, they condemned her as a person: "We write to condemn recent statements our colleague Amy Wax . . . has made in popular media pieces."[26] To be sure, it is not Wax but her statements that are specifically condemned; there is a difference, however, between saying that we strongly disagree with a statement and saying that we condemn it; statements worthy of condemnation are by definition statements that shouldn't have been made, and condemning them is tantamount to condemning the person who made them. Could it be a complete coincidence that within less than two weeks, students belonging to the Penn chapter of the National Lawyers Guild released a statement characterizing Wax's views as "an explicit and implicit endorsement of white supremacy" and urged the dean to take her out of required first-year courses, where neophyte students would be subjected to her "bigoted views"?[27] The dean, Theodore Ruger, declined to do so and defended Wax's right to speak, but he hedged his bets considerably by speaking of her "divisive even noxious views" and announcing that "as a scholar and educator I reject emphatically any claim that a single cultural tradition is better than all others."[28] Wax would reply that she never said that; what she did say, in the op-ed and elsewhere, is that "bourgeois values" like thrift, sexual restraint, and a strong work ethic will better serve citizens who want to flourish in the "advanced economy" of this and other countries. She has been careful to say that these values are not "the property of white people"; the superiority she alleges is cultural, not racial.

Now there is a lot to sort out here (and the story has more chapters to follow) for there are multiple speakers, and what we want to ask is which of them had the right, both legally and professionally, to speak as they did. I have already said that Wax and Alexander had every right to speak out on matters they considered important (a right that is theirs as citizens) and that their colleagues had every right to express their disagreement, although their expression of condemnation may have crossed a line. What about the dean? Well, no provost or president is going to remove him for what he said and no legal liability attaches to his utterances. But there is a professional question: Is a dean more limited in what he can say than the faculty he administers? There is reason to think so. A dean's responsibility is to the smooth running of the enterprise and to an evenhanded concern for the dignity and professional well-being of every faculty member; he or she shouldn't play favorites or create scapegoats. Ruger defaulted on that responsibility when he said, in effect, *Amy Wax has the right to her opinions, but they are divisive and wrong, and I, as dean, reject them.* As an administrator, it's not his job to either reject or endorse the views members of his faculty express; it is his job to affirm the right of the faculty to express them. If Wax's colleagues were wrong to slide from disagreement into moral disapproval, Ruger was doubly wrong when he did the same thing because he forgot entirely what his job was: not to judge faculty sentiments but to protect them. He said that he was speaking "as a scholar," but once he becomes a dean, that posture is no longer available to him. He is always speaking "as a dean," and his words will be received as the words of a dean and not as the words of the faculty member he used to be. Both scholars-turned-deans and the faculty colleagues they have left behind often seem unable to understand what has changed when the title changes. Ruger got it half-right (which puts him one up on most administrators): he was right when he refused to discipline Wax for her constitutionally protected speech; he was wrong when he took pains to disassociate himself from it. Perhaps Ruger had his eye on the different constituencies that might be paying attention to this incident and was trying to strike a stance that would gain the support of as many of them as possible. Wax reports that in a conversation with her, Ruger described himself as a "pluralistic dean" who must accommodate "all sides."[29] I understand that calculation (if he was making it in this instance), but I would maintain that it is the wrong one because it mixes up academic politics with the politics of fund-raising and popular opinion.

You may think this is a quibble and that by and large Dean Ruger acquitted himself well in the situation. But then something else came to light and the story took a turn. In September 2017, Wax was interviewed by a Brown University economist, Glenn Loury. In the course of that interview, she touched on the question of affirmative action and rehearsed what is known as the "mismatch theory." It says that students who lack the raw numerical credentials for admission but are admitted to top-tier universities by affirmative action criteria set themselves up for failure.[30] They find themselves in classes with students whose preparation and skill levels exceed theirs; they struggle to keep up, develop problems with self-esteem, and in general fare less well than they would have had they attended a school to which they would have been admitted by virtue of their test scores.

Had Wax merely rehearsed the mismatch argument (which, needless to say, is controversial) and stopped there she would have been on firm academic ground and there would be no basis at all for rebuke and discipline. But then, as we all sometimes do, she went a bit too far and used her own experience as a longtime teacher of Civil Procedure to buttress her argument. She said, "I don't think I've ever seen a black student graduate in the top quarter and rarely in the top half. I can think of one or two students who scored in the top half in my required first year course. . . . You're putting in front of this person a real uphill battle."[31] Now obviously the point Wax wants to be making centers on "this person"—the minority law student admitted to a school he or she would normally not have gotten into—and the reference to her own experience is somewhat of an aside. Not surprisingly, however, those who were irritated by Wax's position seized on the aside as if it were her main point and declared that her racism was now fully revealed. In response to new calls that Wax be fired or disciplined, Dean Ruger reversed himself and announced that Wax would no longer be teaching first-year students.

Why did he take that action? First, he explained, because Wax's statistics are in error. "Black students," Ruger insists, "have graduated in the top of the class at Penn Law"; moreover, "black students at Penn Law are extremely successful both inside and outside the classroom, in the job market, and in their careers."[32] So far this is merely a scholarly correction. But then Ruger makes two moves whose relationship to each other is problematic. He says that because the law school "does not permit the public disclosure of grades or class rankings . . . or publicize grade performances by racial group," Wax has transgressed a policy of confidentiality. But if Wax's statistics are wrong, as Ruger says they are, she has not disclosed anything (although Ruger now has); she's just made a mistake. Perhaps she was trying to transgress a policy, but she failed to do so.

Ruger, however, has another objection to what she said to Loury, and that objection has more weight: "Black students assigned to her class in the first week at Penn Law may reasonably wonder whether their professor has already come to a conclusion about their presence, performance, and potential for success in law school and thereafter."[33] Much depends on whether this is an empirical or a theoretical matter. Is there evidence that minority students who know about the anti–affirmative action positions of their teachers feel as Ruger says they do? Or is it at least sometimes the case that students are able either to discount or set aside the political positions of their teachers, especially in a course like Civil Procedure that doesn't offer many openings for the introduction of political positions? And if the question is a theoretical one, are we prepared as a matter of general principle to say that anyone who announces a policy position distressing to some identifiable group of students should not be allowed to teach in classrooms populated by members of that group? Strictly enforced, such a dictum would result in very few professors being eligible to teach any classes at all.

The underlying question is whether Ruger is making an academic decision for which he has academic reasons, or is making what only appears to be an academic decision but is really a decision produced within a political calculation. If Ruger is given the benefit of the doubt and we decide that his reason for disciplinary action was academic, he was within his rights and responsibilities to say what he said in his second letter to the Penn Law community. If, however, he spoke with an eye to external constituencies—if he was offering Wax up as a sacrifice to those she had offended—he can be faulted for marching to a political rather than an academic drummer. But however one comes down on the issue, no genuine First Amendment considerations will have been in play. What we have here are professional considerations that happen to involve the production of speech. Did Ruger exceed his mandate when he not only challenged Wax's statistics but implicitly impugned her motives? Was removing her from the first-year classroom an act dictated by the obligations of his office, or was he overreacting and hiding behind the First Amendment, as a Penn Board of Trustees member who resigned thought he did?[34] Did Wax in her turn speak unwisely and perhaps unprofessionally? Is she a racist? The evidence says no, and even if she were, does having racist views disqualify you from teaching in a university? (I think not.) These are genuine questions, but, to repeat my point, they are not First

Amendment questions. The conditions of Wax's employment were altered because of something she said, but she was able to say it freely; no speech right of hers was abridged; and the debate about whether the consequences she suffered were justified is a debate about professional judgment (hers and her dean's) and not a debate about a constitutional principle.

The Steven Salaita Story

Much the same could be said about another case in which free speech issues and professional issues were conflated when they should have been distinguished. This time, the central figure is on the left. Steven Salaita, a professor of English at Virginia Tech University, was offered a tenured position at the University of Illinois, Champaign-Urbana. The offer, which was extended at the end of a nationwide search, was accepted, and in a short time Salaita resigned from Virginia Tech (as did his wife, who was a staff member), sold his house, and began hunting for a place to live in Urbana. Meanwhile, moving expenses had been negotiated, an office was assigned to him, and his courses were put on the schedule. Then, in early August 2014, three weeks before he was to teach his first class, Salaita was told by then chancellor Phyllis Wise that she would not be forwarding his file to the Board of Trustees and that the offer of employment had been withdrawn.

Why was it withdrawn? In the period between the tendering of the offer and its withdrawal, Salaita, known as a pro-Palestinian, anti-Israeli activist, had sent out a series of tweets thought by many to be offensive, scurrilous, outrageous, and anti-Semitic. Here are two of them: "If you're defending Israel now you're an awful human being"; "At this point, if Netanyahu appeared on TV with a necklace made from the teeth of Palestinian children, would anybody be surprised?"[35] There is evidence (although not in the university's official record) that Wise's action was taken in response to pressure from legislators, parents, alumni, and donors. She was careful to say in an August 22 statement that the university was pledged to protect "robust—and even intense and provocative—debate," but she added, "[W]hat we cannot and will not tolerate . . . are personal and disrespectful words or actions that demean and abuse either viewpoints themselves or those who express them."[36] If the "we" referenced here is the university community in general and members of the senior administration in particular, one wonders how far their resolve not to tolerate extends. Salaita did not publish his tweets on a university server or proclaim them on the quad. Why, then, should Wise and her colleagues have *any* official relation to them unless they think of themselves as obliged and authorized to monitor everything everywhere?

I trust it is clear that in at least some ways Salaita and Wax, although on different sides of the political aisle, are similarly situated: both have been denied professional benefits to which they were otherwise entitled because of something they said in a nonacademic setting. The difference is that while Wax was removed from a course she had taught for many years, Salaita never got to teach a class at Illinois at all and, as it turned out, became pretty much unemployable. (In 2017, he announced that he was leaving the academy.) Both uttered sentiments that were controversial because they touched on hot-button issues—racism and anti-Semitism—and both were told by administrators that the content of those sentiments played no part in the action taken against them. Chancellor Wise anticipates Dean Ruger when she declares, "[E]very student must know that every instructor recognizes and values that student as a human being."[37] She's not reacting to Salaita's views, or so she claims; she doesn't want students at Illinois who might sit in Salaita's classes to feel that their teacher doesn't respect them, just as Dean Ruger doesn't want Penn Law School's black students to feel that Amy Wax has come to a conclusion about their abilities before the semester starts. One might argue that Ruger's concern for the welfare of his students has a firmer basis than Wise's. The students he is solicitous of are not the projection of an abstract possibility of psychological harm; if there is an injury to be suffered, they have already suffered it, and, given the demographics of law school student populations, everyone knows who they are. In contrast, Wise's solicitude is for students yet to matriculate and who, because of her action, will never be subject to the disadvantage she imagines.

Nevertheless, despite these differences (and the difference that Penn is a private institution and Illinois a public one), the questions put earlier to the Wax case are apt here. If Salaita was out of line, what line are we talking about: a professional line, a moral line, a legal line? Is what he said in his tweets disqualifying for membership in the academy? Is he an anti-Semite (I don't think so), and if he is, is there a rule (stated or implied) that credentialed professors cannot be anti-Semites? Can we legitimately reason from the off-campus expression of an instructor's political views to his or her performance in the classroom? (Both Wax's and Salaita's student evaluations were full of praise for their dedicated and even-handed teaching.) Is there a political litmus test for entry into the professoriat? Note once again that by and large these are not First Amendment questions but questions about the limitations and obligations of professional behavior. The only constitutional issue in sight is the issue of whether Illinois, a public university, violated Salaita's rights by firing (or de-hiring) him because it didn't like his political views. And that issue is obscured or at least made difficult because (1) arguably, he was never officially hired in the first place (Chancellor Wise cites a boilerplate provision, often ignored, that the finalization of an appointment requires Board of Trustees approval), and (2) according to the university, his politics were not the reason for its action.

The James Tracy Story

The same claim—*We're getting rid of you, but we're not punishing you for your ideas*—was made by the administrators of Florida Atlantic University when in 2016 they fired James Tracy, a tenured professor who, in a series of blogs and other public venues, said that the Sandy Hook tragedy in Newtown, Connecticut, was staged by certain constituencies with the intention of creating a favorable climate for the passage of gun control legislation. Tracy also engaged in a high-profile dispute with Leonid and Veronique Pozner, parents of a six-year-old boy who died in the massacre. The Pozners complained that Tracy's writings caused them incredible pain and anguish and reported having received from him a letter demanding proof that their son Noah actually existed and that they were the persons they purported to be. For his part, Tracy claimed that the Pozners were conspiring to deprive him of his livelihood. He added that if teaching that mass media should be interrogated "is an outmoded ideal and a skill that can no longer be practiced or taught to young adults, I stand guilty as charged."[38]

Tracy's fears proved prophetic. In 2016 he was removed from his position. The university's claim (mirroring the claims of the dean of the Penn Law School and the chancellor of the University of Illinois) was that Tracy was not dismissed for having and/or publishing controversial views but for having failed to fill out forms asking faculty members to report on outside activities for which they received compensation and which might have involved a conflict of interest. Tracy, in turn, asserted that his blog specifically disclaimed any relationship between his views and the views

of Florida Atlantic University.[39] It was his position that there had
been little or no enforcement of the requirement to supply the
disclosure forms regarding possible conflicts of interest and that he
was being singled out for discipline solely because the university
disapproved of his constitutionally protected views. (I can report
that in eighteen years of writing for the *New York Times*, I failed
to fill out similar disclosure forms at four universities and suffered
no repercussions.) That disapproval was in fact voiced in a mass
email by then FAU president Mary Jane Saunders: "I want to make
it clear that those views and opinions are not shared by Florida
Atlantic University, and I am personally saddened by any media
stories that have added to the pain felt by the victims' families."[40]

The question raised here is the same one raised by the Amy
Wax and Steven Salaita incidents: Is it the proper business of a
senior university administrator to express either approval or disapproval of a faculty member's political views? Should FAU, as an
institution, have *any* views on what happened or didn't happen
at Newtown? Saunders's email has the university intervening in
a political debate, something it has no business (a phrase meant
literally) doing, even if, as in this case, the intervention would be
applauded by almost everyone.

President Patricia McGuire of Trinity Washington University
disagrees. In 2017 she wrote a blog post criticizing President
Trump's travel ban and taking special aim at Trinity alumna and
Trump counselor Kellyanne Conway, who, she said, "played a
large role in facilitating . . . the grave injustice being perpetrated
by the Trump administration's war on immigrants." In response
to those who objected that as president she should have stayed
"out of the political circus," McGuire said that "presidents are not
mere spectators," and that when "truth, integrity and justice are at
stake . . . presidents must not shy away from public responses."[41]
At stake where? Everywhere? It would seem so, since McGuire has

apparently given herself a roving commission to speak out publicly and with the authority of her office whenever she thinks truth and justice are being threatened. (Does she wear a cape and a costume?) And I thought that the commission of university presidents was limited to the duties they were hired to perform, duties McGuire trivializes when she accuses her critics of wanting her to "stick to serving tea." Serving tea sometimes, no doubt, when the occasion is ceremonial, but in between ceremonies there are the small tasks of administering a faculty, building a curriculum, maintaining a physical plant, ensuring campus security, managing the budget, overseeing the athletic program, monitoring the office of admissions, presiding over promotion and recruitment, raising funds, and nourishing alumni relationships (Goodbye, Kellyanne Conway). That seems enough to do without taking on the additional tasks assigned to legislatures, the press, the United Nations, and the pope. And where does it end? If as an administrator you feel obliged to disown a faculty member's view on Sandy Hook or rebuke an alumna for her loyalty to Trump, what's to stop you from disowning a faculty member or graduate who speaks out on some other matter—race, gender, the environment, abortion, whatever? This is one time when the slippery-slope argument has force: if you align the university with a position on one public issue, you've opened the door to aligning the university with a position on another, and then another, and then another, and pretty soon you won't have a university at all; you'll have a political message center.

What is true of universities is also true of professional academic associations. In 2016 a group calling itself Historians Against Trump wrote an open letter to the country warning voters about the danger Trump and his possible election posed to the republic.[42] The signatories, including many prominent and distinguished historians, cited their academic credentials as a reason for hearkening to what they had to say. But *as* historians, the letter writers are in

litical speech when in 2018 she called the Trump administration's policy of separating children from their parents at the border with Mexico cruel and immoral?[43] It depends on whether she was speaking as a university administrator or as a former secretary of the Department of Homeland Security. If the latter, then there is nothing to rebuke in her expressing an opinion; she spoke as an expert on the issues raised by Trump's action. But if she spoke as a university administrator—*I am the president of the University of California and here's what I think*—she spoke out of turn if only because millions of Americans, including some of her faculty and students, think something else and blame the children's parents for being at the border in the first place. But, someone might object, couldn't she simply disassociate herself from her academic title and make it clear (as James Tracy tried to) that her views were not the university's? I tend to doubt it; despite disclaimers, many would hear what she said as issuing from the institution of which she is the chief executive officer. Better to not run the risk and refrain from political commentary until you've left your university office. Intervening on the side of the wounded and unfortunate may make you feel good, but it also associates your university with one party to a political battle that has not yet passed into history. Academic administrators should pronounce only on those moral issues so long settled that pronouncement is unnecessary and superfluous.

No one any longer believes that there is a positive case to be made for slavery (although many made it for centuries), but slavery is almost unique as an issue on which there is now only one side. Other political questions are very much alive—questions such as whether Islam is a terrorist religion or whether Israel is an apartheid state or whether the Trump presidency is a threat to democracy. A university has no business expressing a view on those questions or any other questions still being contested. And should a faculty member, in his or her capacity as a citizen, speak out on such a contested matter, the university should not respond in any way, except to reaffirm the faculty member's right to express his or her views even if the view expressed is "Jews bring their troubles on themselves" (uttered by a professor in an off-campus op-ed) or "Blacks just can't make it in elite law schools" (uttered by a professor in an interview). The university should have *nothing* to say about those views, unless they have been urged by a professor in class, in which case that professor has abandoned his or her academic responsibilities and become a political agent. An administration stepping in at that point would still not be taking a stand on the substantive political issues; it would just be censuring an instructor for crossing a line that shouldn't be crossed.

That is what Sweet Briar College instructor Nell Boeschenstein did when on the day after Trump's election she pondered whether she should walk into class and say "[L]et's turn to page 46 and pick up where we left off" or acknowledge the "elephant in the room" and initiate a discussion of Trump's victory.[44] She chose to do the latter. That was her first mistake: she began the class by exchanging its academic focus for a political one. The mistake was compounded when, after prodding her reluctant students, she discovered that a number of them had actually voted for Trump. Immediately she began to harangue them, asking, "Why did you give Trump a pass on the racism, the misogyny. The xenophobia and the environment? . . . Why do you forgive this man's rejection of the fundamental values on which we agree? Please explain this to me." Suddenly students who thought they were in the room to receive instruction were instead on the receiving end of a political lecture that concluded with their being commanded to go forth and "stand up against [Trump's] language of bigotry." The transformation of the occasion from an educational lesson to a political rally was complete, a transformation for which Boeschenstein offered no apology. Indeed her only regret was that she hadn't engineered it earlier in the semester: "Had I been brave enough to start this conversation in September, I wonder whether some of my Trump-supporting students might have chosen otherwise at the ballot box on Tuesday." Or in other words, *I wish that I had abandoned my professional responsibilities sooner.* She should have been disciplined if not dismissed, if only because, by her own admission, she was no longer performing the duties she had been trained and paid to perform and was defaulting on those duties willfully and eagerly.

The same is true of those teaching assistants at the University of North Carolina, Chapel Hill, who, in response to a decision to house a controversial statue commemorating Confederate soldiers in a new building, struck and refused to turn in student grades for the fall 2018 semester. Provost Robert Blouin got it exactly right when he said that withholding grades for a political reason "violates our university's instructional responsibilities." Blouin was particularly distressed to learn that some instructors were using class time to win students to the strikers' side. That, he pointed out, amounted to coercion and "an exploitation of the student-teacher relationship."[45] The instructors who are striking and recruiting undergraduates for their cause should lose their teaching assistantships, for, like Boeschenstein, they are no longer performing as academics.

James Tracy does not seem to fall into this category; he was under fire for the extramural expression of political views, not for turning his classroom into a political forum. The legal issue was cut and dried. As U.S. District Judge Robin Rosenberg said in her instructions to the jury, a state entity cannot dismiss an employee because of his or her constitutionally protected speech, which means speech addressed to a "matter of public concern." Rosenberg also explained that dislike of an employee's protected speech did not have to be the sole reason for disciplinary sanctions; so long as it was a contributing factor, the action would be suspect on constitutional grounds. Despite the judge's charge, the jury took just three hours to decide that Tracy's termination was justified. The jury foreman acknowledged that the cited FAU policies were "inconsistently enforced" but added that "Professor Tracy is a smart guy and he knew what they wanted him to do" and he didn't do it.[46] In other words, Tracy wasn't savvy at playing the game and therefore deserved the consequences. One of Tracy's attorneys, Matthew Benzion, responded by saying, "They [university administrators] didn't like his speech and they wanted him gone." On the record, that seems to be true. (Tracy has now appealed the district court's ruling to the Eleventh Circuit.)

In the three main cases we have examined a key question is whether an instructor's controversial political views informed and, by informing, corrupted his or her pedagogical performance. Only if that corruption had occurred would a disciplinary response by an administration be in order. According to students who sat in Tracy's classroom, he was a demanding and insightful professor who required that they work hard and think hard. There didn't seem to be any complaints that he had turned his academic classroom into a platform for his partisan agenda. Like Wax and Salaita, Tracy was undone by the assumption that an instructor who voices political views many would find objectionable necessarily allows those views to skew his teaching. The record does not seem to bear out this assumption in any of the instances examined in this chapter, and I would contend that there is no necessary relationship between a teacher's political profile and the shape or quality of his or her teaching. Each case must be considered on the basis of the evidence surrounding it. Unfortunately, this is a point that escapes university administrators, who seem unable to understand the necessary distinctions. And that is why the stories of Wax, Salaita, and Tracy constitute a cautionary tale the moral of which is that faculty members who speak out strongly in public venues do so at their own peril, even if their classroom performance is exemplary and what they say is constitutionally protected speech.

Free Speech Is Still Not an Academic Value

Controversies of the kind surveyed in these pages pop up every day. In fact as I write, Brooklyn College is in the middle of one. Business professor Mitchell Langbert, upset by the nomination hearings of Supreme Court Justice Brett Kavanaugh, wrote on his (nonuniversity) blog, "If someone did not commit sexual assault in high school, then he is not a member of the male sex."[47] Immediately there were calls for his dismissal, and just as immediately the college's provost and president defended his free-speech rights but took care to say how appalled they were by what he said. Déjà vu all over again. These administrators just don't understand that the claim to be protecting the free-speech rights of faculty members is undermined when a particular exercise of that right is denounced in the same breath. Harvard administrators did not denounce Ronald Sullivan Jr. when he agreed to join Harvey Weinstein's defense team, but the university did launch a "climate review" of the situation at Winthrop House (the residential college of which he was the faculty dean) so that it could "have a more complete understanding of the current environment." It is "shocking," said Harvard professor Jeannie Suk Gersen, that Harvard is undertaking an official 'review' of the 'climate' arising from Professor Sullivan's professional choice," especially when "the review is not based on an allegation that Professor Sullivan has violated any university policy."[48] The administration seems no more able than the students it administers to make the relevant distinctions.

I could go on adding more and more examples, but there would be no end to it. The full story of free speech on campus will never be written; nevertheless some conclusions can be drawn:

1. Freedom of speech is not an academic value; freedom of inquiry is, and freedom of inquiry requires the silencing of voices. The demand, voiced by many students and some commentators, that the entire university be a "free-speech zone" misconceives the enterprise, which is not freedom of speech but education. Given that so many university administrators endorse and make the same mistake, it is not surprising that Donald Trump threatens to "require colleges to support free speech if they want federal research money."[49] Underlying his threat is the assumption misguided administrators allow to flourish, the assumption that research and free speech are the same thing or are even distantly related. University administrative cowardice is reaping its own bad reward.

2. The supposed conundrums that arise when controversial speakers are invited to campus give rise to no genuine free-speech issues but for the most part reduce to questions of administrative competence and the recognition (or misrecognition) by administrators of what their job is.

3. Student protestors take themselves out of First Amendment territory and out of the educational process altogether when they refuse dialogue and stand pat on a conviction of virtue so strong that it precludes listening to what anyone else has to say and leads to acts of obstruction and violence.

4. Free-speech issues may be implicated when something an academic says leads to a negative alteration in the conditions of employment, but even in those situations professional considerations are often more relevant than legal or constitutional ones.

I believe these conclusions to be correct, but I must acknowledge that they are out of step with the conventional wisdom as represented by a committee of the Faculty Senate of the University of Minnesota. The committee produced a report titled "Free Speech at the University of Minnesota" (2016) in which it was said that (1) "the University of Minnesota's Board of Regents' policy guarantees the freedom to speak or write as a public citizen without institutional restraint or discipline"; (2) "a public university must be absolutely committed to protecting free speech both for constitutional and academic reasons"; (3) "no member of the university community has the right to prevent or disrupt expression"; and (4) "even when protecting free speech conflicts with other important university values, free speech is paramount."[50]

Every one of these statements is false. If the university were to guarantee the freedom to speak without institutional restraint or discipline, it would cease to be a university because it would have replaced the academic value of freedom of inquiry with the constitutional value of freedom of expression; they are not the same, and they are not compatible. Moreover, there are *no* academic reasons for absolutely protecting free speech, and whatever constitutional reasons there are have been declared by the courts to be outweighed by professional reasons, that is, by the imperatives that arise from the educational enterprise. (See the line of cases including *Tinker v. Des Moines, Pickering v. Board of Education, Connick v. Myers, Garcetti v. Ceballos.*[51]) As for preventing expression, that's the assigned task (as I noted at the beginning of this chapter) of departments, deans, provosts, and journal editors; saying who can and cannot speak is their job. And, finally, when free-speech values conflict with university values, university values should win every time. If they don't, it's because senior administrators can't seem to think clearly about these matters. This is perhaps not surprising, but it is certainly depressing and it suggests that universities will be unable to extricate themselves from the free-speech controversies they have largely invented by failing to recognize that their primary obligation is not to the First Amendment but to the maintenance of the enterprise whose flourishing is their one and only task.

CHAPTER 4

Why the Religion Clause of the First Amendment Doesn't Belong in the Constitution

Is Religion Special?

Religious speech is a source of controversy because it is often ut-tered without the silent caveat *This is what I think; you may think something else; let's talk* that accompanies words spoken in a liberal state where the bottom-line assumption is that matters are never completely settled. Religions, at least theistic ones like Judaism, Christianity, and Islam, offer themselves not as one way to truth among others but as the true way in relationship to which other ways are false paths. No one likes to be told that his or her way of life is false or sinful, and anyone told that will feel that those saying such things are speaking hate. Religious speakers will reply that they are bound by the dictates of their faith and mean no harm to any-one ("We hate the sin but love the sinner"); it is just that they have no choice in the matter. For the believer, religion's commands are uncompromising even when obeying them involves discriminating on the basis of gender, religion, race, and sexual orientation. And so we get to the typical Religion Clause case, where a believer requests an exemption from a generally applicable law (a law directed at everyone, not an individual or particular group) on the reasoning that conforming to the law would involve performing or failing to perform acts either forbidden or commanded by his or her faith.

Reynolds v. United States is an early example that presages many of today's controversies.[1] George Reynolds, a Mormon who had been convicted of bigamy, defended himself by pointing out that according to his religion, the penalty for refusing to practice polygamy "would be damnation in the life to come." The Court rejected this defense and its underlying assumption that "religious belief can be accepted as a justification of an overt act made criminal by the law of the land." Were we to accept this justification, the Court concluded, the result "would be to make the professed doctrines of religious belief superior to the law of the land, and in effect to permit every citizen to become a law unto himself." One hundred thirty years later, some county clerks, florists, photographers, and bakers are making Reynolds's arguments all over again, and all over again courts are faced with the task of reconciling two lines of argument—God's will is paramount, and no, it isn't—that cannot be reconciled. George Reynolds wanted to be able to say "I do" serially. Kim Davis, a county clerk in Kentucky, didn't want to issue a marriage license to anyone who wanted to say "I do" to someone of the same sex. The law said no to both of them, and the question is *How could it do so and still claim to be upholding religious freedom?* Is religious speech less free than secular speech because some courts silence it when its effect is discriminatory? Or is religious speech more free than secular speech because in some other courts it can be successfully invoked as a counterweight to the obligation to treat everyone equally?

These questions animate this chapter and point the way to an understanding of its odd title. After all, what could I possibly mean by saying that the Religion Clause doesn't belong in the Constitution? Everyone knows that the desire for religious freedom motivated many of those who left Europe and came to what was called the New Jerusalem. Supreme Court Justice Hugo Black rehearsed the familiar story in *Everson v. Board of Education*: "A large proportion of the early settlers of this country came here . . . to escape the bondage of laws which compelled them to support and attend government favored churches."[2] So there are sound historical reasons for the inclusion of a clause forbidding Congress to establish a state religion or to place burdens on the religious free exercise of citizens. I don't of course intend to deny that history or to reopen the eighteenth-century debates between federalists and antifederalists about the wisdom of having a bill of rights at all. My point is conceptual rather than historical. However the Religion Clause got into the Constitution, we can still ask whether the principles it announces fit with the more general principles informing the entire document. I will argue that they do not.

The Religion Clause says that "Congress shall make no law respecting an establishment of religion, or prohibiting the free exercise thereof." There are two directives here. The first says that the state cannot establish a religious orthodoxy, and the second says that you and I are entitled freely to exercise our religion. We call these two clauses the Establishment Clause and the Free Exercise Clause, respectively. Naming them does nothing to settle them down, for we must determine exactly what they mean, a task that is ongoing to this day. But before we take up that task yet again, we must pose a prior question: What exactly is meant by "religion"? In the absence of a definition of religion, it's hard to see how you would set about reasoning when a Religion Clause case came up. Here is a definition that was put forward in the Universal Military

Training and Service Act of 1958. After stating that those who object to service in the armed forces on the basis "of religious training and belief" will be exempt, the act defined religious training and belief as follows: "Religious training and belief . . . means an individual's belief in relation to a Supreme Being involving duties superior to those arising from any human relation, but does not include essentially political, sociological or philosophic views or a merely personal moral code." So to qualify for an exemption, you must believe in a God whose commands supersede the commands of any earthly authority, and that belief must be acquired in the course of "religious training," training administered by something like a church which comes complete with doctrines, rituals, ecclesiastical hierarchies, criteria for entry and expulsion, and so on. That was for a long time the commonsense definition of "religion" (and still is for many), and we can assume, I think, that it is the definition the framers of the Constitution had in mind.

The point is important because the way the Religion Clause is interpreted will depend on what definition of religion is in place. The scope of the Free Exercise Clause, for example, will be quite large if religious exercise is understood to include the performance of "duties superior to those arising from any human relation." Read strongly, that means that when there is a clash between earthly, secular duties and a duty one owes to God, the duty owed to God wins. This was certainly Abraham's understanding when he obeyed without question God's command to sacrifice his only son "for a burnt offering."[3] The example may seem extreme (and of course God stayed Abraham's hand), but it can stand in for all those moments when there is a conflict between human obligations, including familial, legal, institutional, political, and even moral ones, and the obligation to deity.

In *United States v. Seeger* and *Welsh v. United States*, the Supreme Court relaxed the Universal Military Training and Service

Act's definition of religion and let in everything the act excluded when it came up with a new test for conscientious objection: "namely does the claimed belief occupy the same place in the life of the objector as an orthodox belief in God holds in the life of one clearly qualified for exemption"?[4] In short, political, philosophical, and merely personal views now count too. In a troubled concurrence to *Welsh*, Justice Harlan observed that the Court's new test completely ignores and overrides the act's "distinction between theistic and nontheistic religions." In so doing, the Court "has performed a lobotomy and completely transformed the statute." It has also made the conscientious objection test difficult to administer: what was once a clear, if parochial, requirement—belief in God acquired through religious training—has now become a requirement so loose that almost anything in the way of strong commitment (or asserted strong commitment) might meet it as long as it was "sincere, honest, and made in good faith."[5]

Determining whether those conditions have been satisfied opens up a new can of legal worms; one might ask what exactly does a Court bent on decentering and dislodging traditional religious practice mean by the phrase "good faith." By its reasoning any faith from any source is good. Once you soften the distinction between religious commitments and commitments grounded in philosophy or personal opinion, it is hard to see what the Religion Clause means or if it means anything since religion is no longer identifiable by features that distinguish it from other discourses What's the logic in protecting something by denying to it its core content? As law professor Michael Stokes Paulsen explains, "Religious liberty simply does not make sense on purely secular grounds that start from the premise that sincere religious conviction does not correspond to anything real."[6] Yet that's the premise underlying the expanded definition of religion: we broaden what we mean by religion so that the word does not refer to a specific doctrinal commitment, but to a degree of conviction anyone can feel about anything. Folding religious obligations into the category of obligations strongly felt by both religious and nonreligious persons leaves us with the vocabulary of free exercise and nonestablishment but with no clear referents for its terms. The *Seeger* and *Welsh* courts deal with the awkward category of religious affirmation—awkward because by the logic of liberalism religious affirmation should be no different from any other—by generalizing it out of existence, a strategy that later becomes an art under the rubric of "pluralism."

I bring up *Seeger* and *Welsh* at the outset because they raise a question readers will likely be asking: What religion or whose religion do I have in mind when I talk in this chapter about the demands religion makes on its adherents in the context of conflicts between civic and religious duties? The religion that takes the Abraham-like form of a total fidelity to transcendent command, or the softer religion (if it is a religion at all) whose commands are looser and more diffuse and therefore more available to being harmonized with the secular protocols of the liberal state? In general, I shall be taking as a model the more severe religiosity of those who will not relax their obligations of faith for a moment. I do this because the uncompromising model sharpens the issues that animate current disputes between, for example, those merchants who refuse in the name of the free exercise of religion to lend their skills to the celebration of a same-sex marriage, and those who argue that the state's commitment to eliminating discrimination outweighs free exercise rights. The opposing positions on this and other issues will be tied to opposing views of what religion is. Those who put forward strong free exercise claims insist on the unique, categorical nature of the obligations their religion imposes on them and argue that, properly understood, the clause mandates accommodations that exempt them from what are otherwise generally applicable laws. Those who would limit free exercise and grant few if any accommodations deny the uniqueness of religious obligations and analogize them to obligations nonreligious persons also feel; the question of accommodation need never arise. One party is saying religion is special and must be treated as such; the other is saying that it is not special and that the liberal state can be fair to religion—or to a religion recast in liberalism's terms—even if religion's deepest claim, the claim to be supreme in authority, is denied. Exploring these issues will be the business of this chapter.

Religion and the Liberal State

Now that we have gotten the question of defining religion out of the way (by fudging it), we can take up another question that should be considered before we look at particular cases. Why is there a Religion Clause in the Constitution anyway? I ask that question because in both its spirit and its details the Constitution is a liberal document, by which I mean it follows and extends the principles of Enlightenment liberalism, principles that mandate the protection of individual rights, including the right to free speech, the right to petition, and the right of a press to be free of government interference. These are all rights held by citizens against the state that might wish to curtail or suppress them. In other, nonliberal, forms of government, rights belong to the state or to a monarch or to the church or to a collective, and citizens are asked to subordinate their views, preferred agendas, or life aspirations to the larger entity. Liberalism makes that larger entity the servant of the individual rather than the other way around. It is the individual's choices that must be honored and protected, and the state is prohibited from making choices for him or her or speaking for him or her. It follows, then, that while the key value in other political systems is obedience or conformity, the key value in the liberal scheme of government is individual freedom, and that means individual choice—the choice of what to think, of what to say, of where to pray or not to pray, of whom to associate with, and so on. To be sure, "freedom of choice" does not include the choice to perform criminal acts; no state could countenance generally unlawful behavior and still be in any sense a state. But within the very large category of acts that are not labeled criminal by statutes, the individual is, by and large, free. That freedom is equally distributed, which means that the state's protection must be extended without favor. It cannot be stipulated in advance that the speech or ideas or religious views of some citizens are valued or devalued more than the speech or ideas or religious views (or antireligious views) of other citizens. No list of preferred or dis-preferred viewpoints—religious, political, or any other—should be kept by the administrators of the liberal state.

But here's the rub: the Religion Clause of the First Amendment names both a preferred and a dis-preferred view, and it is the same one. The Free Exercise Clause prefers religion when it forbids the state to burden religious free exercise. There is a long-standing debate as to whether "free exercise" includes actions inspired by religious commitments or is limited to thinking and expressing religious thoughts. If it is the latter, the clause seems superfluous since the right to think and speak your mind is already guaranteed by the Free Expression Clause; if it is the former—if it is religiously inspired *acts* that the state cannot sanction—we run into the danger of having an act judged lawful if it was performed in obedience to a religious tenet, and unlawful if it was performed by a nonbeliever for a secular reason. We shall return to this tension (more akin to a contradiction), but for the time being it is enough to note that, however it is interpreted, the Free Exercise Clause pays special attention to religiously inspired deeds, verbal or physical, and that is a nonliberal and nondemocratic thing to do.

The Establishment Clause also singles out religion for special attention, but the attention is negative. Nothing the state does should tend to—play a role in—the establishment of an official religion. The state should not compose prayers to be recited by public school students. The state should not tie public employment to the affirmation of a religious belief. The state, said James Madison in his "Memorial and Remonstrance against Religious Assessments" (1785), should not require citizens to contribute even "three pence" to the support of a religious institution. (This severe stricture has been relaxed to the point where at least one Supreme Court justice complained that the Establishment Clause has been written out of the Constitution, but that is a story for another book.) The Establishment Clause asks the courts to be alert to those moments when something the government says or does, perhaps in all innocence, so entangles it in religious affairs that the wall of separation between church and state is breached. The phrase "wall of separation" is not in the Constitution but appears in a letter written by Thomas Jefferson to the Danbury Baptists in 1802. An even earlier version of the doctrine was laid out by John Locke in "A Letter Concerning Toleration" (1689). To the civil magistrate is left the care of the material world—"outward things such as money, land, houses, furniture and the like"—while to the church and her ministers belongs "the care of the salvation of men's souls." This division of labor is reflected in a state with two realms, the public and the private. In the public realm the laws of property, contract, and financial transactions are understood to rule. In the private realm—the realm of the home, church, chapel, and heart—one is ruled by the obligations set down in the scriptures or written in the believer's heart by the pencil of the Holy Spirit. The task, says Locke, is to ensure that the integrity of each realm is maintained: "He jumbles heaven and earth together . . . who mixes these societies, which are in their original end, business, and in everything, perfectly distinct."

The borders between these two "societies" must be patrolled, and one of the vehicles of "mixing" or "jumbling" is religious speech, which, in certain forms, can constitute a breach of the dividing line by aligning the state with a religious view or purpose. A succession of cases is concerned with asking whether that line has been crossed, and the answers that emerge constitute a jurisprudence that is quite often bewildering. As we survey a few of those cases, it is important to remember that they exist only because of the anomaly of a form of speech that has been labeled "special" (in both positive and negative ways) in a liberal regime whose first principle is that no form of speech is inherently special. Were we faithful to the logic and spirit of liberalism, religious speech would be treated like any other form of speech—no better, no worse. But there is a continuing pressure, cultural and political, to accord religion a special place, and when the Constitution seems to be saying, "No you can't do that," the state and the courts will contrive to do what the Constitution forbids, and the labors performed in the service of this contrivance will be acrobatic and at times breathtaking. As we examine those labors, remember that they are necessary only because the Religion Clause stands in an awkward relationship to the liberal spirit of the Constitution. Religion Clause jurisprudence is by and large an effort to remove that awkwardness by reconciling the demands of liberal tolerance and pluralism with the demands of doctrinal fidelity. That effort will always fail.

When Is a Crèche a Crèche?

One form that effort takes is to de-religionize religious speech. Suppose you are walking past a county courthouse and see on the top of its staircase a Christmas tree adorned with a cross. What will you make of it? Will you think "Here is the state paying tribute to Christianity," or will you think "What a nice tribute to the holiday season"? The question might seem odd—of course the state is here acknowledging the centrality of a religion and marking the birth of its founder. But what seems obvious in ordinary life is not so in Supreme Court cases. Consider *Lynch v. Donnelly*, a 1984 landmark case that exhibits much of the complexity and, indeed, oddity, of Religion Clause decisions.[7] The question at the heart of the case is what, if anything, is being said by the city of Pawtucket, Rhode Island, when it annually mounts a Christmas display at the center of which is a crèche—a tableau consisting of the figures of Jesus, Mary, and Joseph, various angels, shepherds and kings, and a collection of appropriately adoring animals. A number of Pawtucket residents brought a cause of action alleging that the crèche violates the Establishment Clause because it has the appearance of "affiliating the city with the Christian beliefs that the crèche represents." A court of appeals affirmed the district court's judgment in favor of those protesting the display, but the Supreme Court reversed. The Court admits that "the crèche may well have special meaning to those whose faith includes the celebration of religious Masses," but argues that the main purpose of erecting it is to "serve commercial interests and benefit merchants and their employees." The argument is that the crèche facilitates the flow of money into the city of Pawtucket. The religious significance it has for some persons is regarded as incidental and is subordinated to the goal of engendering a "friendly community spirit of good will in keeping with the season." To be sure, the government speaks through the crèche, but it doesn't say "Join us in worship"; rather it says "Join us in spending." This judgment is delivered without irony, even though one city official explained that he favored the display of the crèche because it would further his interest in keeping Christ in Christmas.

Although the majority's reasoning might seem strange and even bizarre, it will seem less so if it is read in the context of a history in which the separation of church and state, supposedly the official posture of the government, has been honored more in the breach than in the observance. As the *Lynch* majority reminds us, in the very week that Congress approved the Establishment Clause, "it enacted legislation providing for paid Chaplains of the House and the Senate," and of course there are coins that bear the motto "In God We Trust" and, since 1954, a Pledge of Allegiance that includes the phrase "under God." These official actions indicate an unwillingness to take the separation of church and state so seriously that every vestige or hint of religion must be scrubbed from the public square. The public display of the crèche, the majority maintains, is nothing more than an "acknowledgment of our religious heritage." To be sure, a crèche would seem to be undeniably a religious symbol, but the Court finds that its religious meaning has been diminished by its appearance in a tableau celebrating "the holiday season." (Apparently the justices forgot the etymology of "holiday.") All the city of Pawtucket has done is take "note of a significant historical religious event long celebrated in the Western World"; it's the history, not any doctrinal content, that is being affirmed. The crèche does not actively exhort us to believe in Christ as the Son of God and our Savior; it is only "a passive symbol" put to a thoroughly secular use, and it has no meaning apart from the encouragement of commercial activity. Mary, Joseph, and the baby Jesus could have been any small family welcoming the opening of a department store.

If you are surprised, and perhaps distressed, by the removal from a Christian symbol of its Christian significance, you have company in the dissenting opinions. Justice William Brennan (joined by Justices Thurgood Marshall, Harry Blackmun, and John Paul Stevens) roundly declared that "the 'primary effect' of including a nativity scene in the city's display is . . . to place the government's imprimatur of approval on the particular religious beliefs exemplified by the crèche." If the display of the crèche is government speech, as it surely is, then what the speech is saying, Brennan insists, is "[H]ere is a truth . . . we as citizens are called to witness." Were the city to be interested only in "celebrating the holiday" and "promoting both retail sales and good will," its purpose could have been effected by the depiction of Santa Claus, reindeer, and wishing wells: "[T]he nativity scene, unlike every other element of the Hodgson Park display, reflects a sectarian exclusivity that the avowed purposes of celebrating the holiday season and promoting retail commerce simply do not encompass." What is encompassed and urged on the viewer, according to the dissent, is that "a divine Savior was brought into the world and that the purpose of this miraculous birth was to illuminate a path towards salvation and redemption." The reduction of that religious message to a commercial one is a piece of transubstantiation Brennan refuses to participate in. He is protesting against a version of the strategy we have already seen deployed in the *Seeger* and *Welsh* cases: defuse the conflict between the singling out for special attention of religious speech and the supposed neutrality of the Constitution toward all forms of expression by draining the religious speech of its religious significance. Transform an exemption from military service based on religious observance into an exemption available to anyone who believes something; transform an obviously religious display into a piece of holiday advertising. What a move!

The Crèche, the Menorah, and the Christmas Tree

Some municipalities have devised another strategy by which religious symbols can find an honored place in the public square without raising constitutional anxieties: just multiply them so that no one of them has precedence or is taken seriously in its own right. The mechanics of this strategy are fully, even comically on display in *County of Allegheny v. ACLU*.[8] A Roman Catholic group placed a crèche on the grand staircase of the Allegheny County Courthouse in downtown Pittsburgh. A block away, outside the entrance to the City-County Building, stood a forty-five-foot-tall Christmas tree. At the foot of the tree was a sign bearing the mayor's name and the inscription "Salute to Liberty." At a certain point an eighteen-foot-high menorah was placed next to the tree. Do either or both of these displays constitute an Establishment Clause violation? Is Pittsburgh affirming the truth of Christianity or Judaism or affirming religion over irreligion?

Justice Blackmun gives crisp answers to these questions. Because the crèche "stands alone" on the staircase, "the county sends an unmistakable message that it supports and promotes the Christian praise to God that is the creche's religious message." But because the menorah "stands next to a Christmas tree and a sign saluting liberty," it is unlikely that "residents of Pittsburgh will perceive the combined display . . . as an 'endorsement' or 'disapproval' . . . of their individual religious choices." Therefore, "for purposes of the Establishment Clause, the city's overall display must be understood as conveying the city's secular recognition of . . . the winter-holiday season." So crèche, no, and menorah-tree-sign, yes.

Wait a minute, say Justices Brennan, Marshall, and Stevens. No matter what other symbols accompany it, "the Christmas tree's religious dimensions could not be overlooked by observers"; moreover, an eighteen-foot-high menorah "would be far more eye-catching" and is "indisputably a religious symbol." Perhaps the two standing side by side removes the possibility that the state is endorsing the message of either, but nothing "permits us to conclude that governmental promotion of religion is acceptable so long as one religion is not favored." The Establishment Clause demands "neutrality, not just among religions, but between religion and non-religion." So if you say no to the crèche, you must say no to the tree and menorah.

That's all wrong, announce Justices Anthony Kennedy, William Rehnquist, Byron White, and Antonin Scalia. We should say yes to both the crèche and the tree-menorah. The Establishment Clause has always permitted "government some latitude in recognizing and accommodating the central role religion plays in our society." If the accommodation does not involve active proselytizing on the part of the state, "the risk of infringement of religious liberty by passive or symbolic accommodation is minimal." Were we to decide otherwise, we would be expressing "an unjustified hostility toward religion, a hostility inconsistent with our precedents." Therefore, crèche yes and tree/menorah yes.

In the end, then, every available answer to the questions of record (except crèche, yes; tree and menorah, no) has been confidently asserted by equally learned and credentialed justices. Of course many Supreme Court opinions display a range of disparate views, but the disparity between the views rehearsed in this one seems more like an abyss. How do we account for it? Part of the answer is to be found in the ultimately incompatible directives given to the courts by the Religion Clause. In one breath (the Free Exercise Clause) the Religion Clause confers a special positive status on religion and in the next (the Establishment Clause) tells the state to stay away from it. As a result, the Court has the impossible task of maneuvering between two conflicting obligations. It is assigned the job of determining the limits of religion (in this case with respect to the appearance of religious symbols in public spaces), but it is warned by the Constitution to keep its distance from religious matters. It can do the job only by ignoring the warning. The Court cannot patrol a border whose lines it is incompetent to draw without engaging in the very trespassing it has been forbidden to engage in. The double command is *Protect it, but keep hands off.* Talk about a catch-22!

How the Liberal State Gets Around the Religion Clause

The way out of this dilemma is truly ingenious: the state contrives to turn religious speech into secular speech, and once that transformation has been effected, the state is free to deal with the speech *as* speech and has been relieved of the puzzles that arise when religion is squarely in the picture. We have already seen one way of pulling off this trick, in *Lynch*: redescribe the religious speech as commercial speech. We have seen another way in *Allegheny*: increase the number of religious symbols—not just a crèche, but a crèche, a dreidel, and a medicine man's lance—so that they become items in a museum rather than candidates for our embrace. The focus is anthropological rather than theological: *Here are some of the ways our citizens worship; you needn't take any of them seriously.* It is by this reasoning that the state can permit religious symbols on public grounds or put the words "In God We Trust" on coins, as long as it is clear that those symbols and words have been emptied of their religious connotations. The vocabulary and symbols of religion can be appropriated without engaging in religious speech if that vocabulary has been employed so often on public occasions that it has become "part of the fabric of our society."[9] After many repetitions, words originally religious carry no more religious significance than the phrase "Good God!," by which we typically mean not that God is good or even that there is a God, but that what has just happened is surprising.

The name Yale Law School's dean Eugene Rostow gave this practice of making religious speech safe for democracy is "ceremonial deism." That phrase is defined by Justice Brennan in his dissent in *Lynch* as a collection of practices that have "lost through rote repetition any significant religious content." The (perhaps counterintuitive) implication is that if you say "God" enough times and on enough public occasions, it will cease to mean "God." In *Elk Grove Unified School District v. Newdow* Justice Sandra Day O'Connor argued that the widespread use of the phrase "under God" and its repeated rehearsal in the Pledge of Allegiance since 1954 turn it into an act of patriotism rather than one of worship.[10] Such phrases, she explained, "can serve to solemnize an occasion instead of to invoke divine providence." The notion of "solemnizing" is another vehicle by means of which the invocation of religious language can at once be engaged in and denied. Yes, the words we are intoning do have their source in religious traditions, but we characteristically use them only to indicate that this occasion is an important one; we solemnize it.

The Court's most sophisticated strategy for secularizing (or laundering) religious speech is to foreground those parts of it that are shared by secular speech and downplay or bracket its doctrinal content. You can then affirm the speech's constitutionality on purely secular grounds and bypass the problem of religion in the public square entirely. Again Locke provides the template in his example of Meliboeus, who owns a calf and wishes to kill it and offer it as a sacrifice to his god. Locke reduces the issue to the right of a property owner to deal with his property as he sees fit and concludes that just as Meliboeus may kill his calf in order to serve it at his dinner table, so may he kill it in order to propitiate his deity. "What may be spent on a feast may be spent on a sacrifice."[11]

Locke then imagines a situation in which, for public health reasons, the state forbids all slaughter of animals. This, he says, is perfectly unobjectionable, for the state is not intentionally regulating Meliboeus's religious performance; rather, it is restricting a general activity which just happens to be put to religious uses by some persons: "In this case the law is not made about a religious, but a political matter: nor is the sacrifice, but the slaughter of calves, thereby prohibited." The ordinance forbidding animal slaughter may impede religious observance, but that's okay because that was not the intention informing it. Once a religious activity or a form of religious speech has been turned into just another secular option—serving up the calf for dinner and laying the calf on an altar are essentially the same; erecting a crèche is an act no different from the installation of a sleigh with reindeer—the state's right to regulate is secure from any Establishment Clause challenge. The political theorist Cécile Laborde provides a contemporary example. A law making motorcycle helmets compulsory negatively impacts "Sikh motorcyclists who wear a turban," but because the law does not single out Sikhs and has as its *general* purpose the promotion of health and safety, its effect of burdening Sikhs is incidental and does not constitute religious discrimination.[12] The Sikh motorcyclist was denied his right to declare his religious affiliation by wearing a turban, but because the denial was not motivated by hostility to his religion, it is not an instance of silencing his religious speech. In the context of this example, the motorcyclist is not a Sikh at all: he's just a generic motorcyclist whose religiosity is beside the secular point of promoting public safety.

Each of these strategies—multiplying religious symbols so that none of them is taken seriously, declaring that certain symbols and phrases have long since shed any religious significance, focusing on those aspects of religious speech and action that are also found in secular speech and action—plays its part in the grand project of making religion safe for the public sphere. (The only area in which the project fails is school prayer: from *Engel v. Vitale* to *Santa Fe Independent School District v. Doe*, courts consistently reject attempts to save school prayer by removing from it any traces of theology or by attributing authorship to students rather than to the state.[13]) To the extent that this project has been successful, one might think that the result would be pleasing to believers. But the success comes with a cost. A religion that has been sanitized for general public use by removing from it the doctrinal tenets a secular state cannot affirm is a religion entirely defanged and, in effect, neutered. Religion is given a place at the table, but in a form that poses no threat to liberal tolerance because the claim to have a source in divinity has been set aside. The liberal state can accommodate religious speech as long as it relaxes any assertion of precedence, as long as it does not present itself as *commanding* the table and arrogating to itself the right to distinguish between the true and the false.

Laborde explains the logic: religious assertions of the kind "God wants us to do X" cannot, she says, form the basis of reasons offered in the public square because such reasons would be unintelligible and inaccessible to nonbelieving citizens. Laborde refers to reasons the liberal state cannot take seriously as "religious reasons *stricto sensu*."[14] In a strict sense, religious reasons derive from and assert a religion's core doctrinal tenets, including of course the tenet that God is the ultimate source of wisdom. No such appeal to "extra-human sources of authority" has a place in liberalism's forum. But if religious discourse is "stripped" (Laborde's word) of any claim of ultimate authority, it becomes dissolved into the mix of possible and plural repositories of wisdom and is thereby legitimized as a participant in the secular process of decision-making. Properly diminished, religion gets the liberal Good Housekeeping Seal of Approval.

But a religion so stripped of its doctrinal content will be of little interest to the strong believer who is pledged to the "strict sense" of his or her faith and will likely disdain a domesticated version of it. What does the liberal state say to believers who, told that their religious views are fine as long as they do not follow them too strictly, reply, "No, thank you, you're asking me to trade my God for yours"? That question, always lurking in the background of Religion Clause jurisprudence, comes front and center when some county clerks, bakers, florists, and photographers refuse to relax the dictates of their faith even when they are in conflict with generally applicable laws. The state is then presented with an unhappy choice: either it can cede some of its authority to strong believers and run the risk of making the individual the judge of which laws to obey, or it can stand firm and be accused of abrogating the free exercise rights of its citizens. Is there a middle way? Liberal theorists like Laborde think so, but the formulas they devise, rather than being "fair" to religion—always liberalism's claim—end up once again marginalizing it in familiar ways, either by removing the religious content from religious speech and action (as Laborde does) or by accommodating only those parts of religion that fit with the secular values of equal respect and nondiscrimination or by denying that a particular legal obligation is really a free exercise burden at all. Sometimes, it is said, religious persons are just oversensitive and imagine infringements on their faith where there are none.

Kim Davis and Compelled Speech

This last was one of the objections made to the behavior of Kim Davis, an elected clerk in Rowan County, Kentucky, who in the summer of 2015 declined to issue marriage licenses to same-sex couples because her religion defines marriage as a union between a man and a woman. (The Supreme Court had recently constitutionalized same-sex marriage in *Obergefell v. Hodges*.[15]) A federal district judge, David Bunning, issued a temporary stay barring Davis from saying no to future same-sex marriage requests. Religious faith, he said, is "not a viable defense" for her actions; public officials cannot be allowed "to choose what orders they follow" just because their religion tells them to. The U.S. Court of Appeals for the Sixth Circuit refused to extend the stay to allow time for an appeal, declaring, "There is . . . little or no likelihood that the clerk in her official capacity will prevail on appeal."[16] When the Supreme Court refused to hear her appeal, Davis said, "I never imagined a day like this would come, where I would be asked to violate a central teaching of Scripture and of Jesus Himself regarding marriage. To issue a marriage license which conflicts with God's definition of marriage, with my name affixed to the certificate, would violate my conscience." "With my name affixed" is the key phrase: she doesn't want to be the means or vehicle of a statement of approval for an action her religion condemns.

Some of Davis's critics argued that her conscience had not in fact been violated because, as Judge Bunning said, she still "may continue to attend Church twice a week, participate in Bible Study and minister to female inmates." One law professor said that Davis's religious liberty rights were not really at stake because "all she's asked to do with couples that come before her is certify that they've met the state requirements for marriage."[17] A prominent gay rights attorney said that Davis just wanted "to use a religious liberty argument to discriminate," despite the fact that "she swore an oath to uphold the Constitution."[18] (Perhaps the attorney forgot that the Free Exercise Clause is part of that Constitution.) These critics were instructing Davis in the proper parameters of her belief: *You can affix your signature to these licenses and still be faithful to your religious convictions, which have other outlets not in conflict with the requirements of your office. In short, let us tell you what your religious obligations are.* It is hardly surprising that Davis proved unreceptive to this counsel. She wasn't interested in the intermittent practice of her faith or in a compromised version of it. She wanted to live her faith out at every moment. She wanted to say yes to God, which in her mind required her to say no to same-sex couples. She didn't want her speech to be compelled in either direction: she didn't want to confirm by her signature a policy her faith abhors, and she didn't want to be silenced by being deprived of the opportunity to affirm her beliefs in public. (In the end, a new governor cut the Gordian knot by removing clerks' names from the licenses issued by their office.)

The doctrine of compelled speech—the government can't tell you what to say or what not to say—plays a large role in those cases that pit free exercise rights against laws that label as criminal acts which religious persons feel obliged to perform. (The law doesn't directly target the acts, but sweeps them up in its general scope.) This doctrine was established in *West Virginia State Board of Education v. Barnette* and *Wooley v. Maynard*.[19] *Barnette* overruled an earlier opinion requiring schoolchildren to recite the Pledge of Allegiance. The Court observed, "To sustain the compulsory flag salute we are required to say that a Bill of Rights which guards the individual's right to speak his own mind, left it open to public authorities to compel him to utter what is not in his mind." This the Court declined to do, noting that "the compulsory flag salute and pledge requires affirmation of a belief." Although efforts "to coerce uniformity of sentiment . . . have been waged by many good as well as by evil men," such efforts find no sanction in the Constitution.

In *Wooley* the compelled affirmation is less direct; it takes the form of a requirement that every automobile bear a license plate. In New Hampshire, the license plate was embossed with the state motto, "Live Free or Die," an unexceptionable sentiment for most Americans but one resisted by those Jehovah's Witnesses who found it repugnant to their beliefs. George Maynard, one of the appellees, put it this way: "I refuse to be coerced into advertising a slogan which I find morally, ethically, religiously and politically abhorrent." The Court observed that Maynard was being compelled to use his private property as a " 'mobile billboard' announcing the state's ideological message" and concluded that no matter how generally acceptable that message might be, the state's interest in conveying it "cannot outweigh an individual's First Amendment right to avoid becoming the courier for such a message."

The Photographer and the Baker

But the decision doesn't always go that way. In recent free exercise cases, the courts (at least the lower courts) have sided with the state and against those who claim an exemption from its generally applicable laws. These days the claim of exemption is being made by religious persons for whom fidelity to their faith means not complying with the anti-discrimination mandate that emerged when same-sex marriage was constitutionalized in *Obergefell v. Hodges*. This development was anticipated by Chief Justice John Roberts when he predicted, in his *Obergefell* dissent, that the "new right to same-sex marriage" would come into conflict with the right to exercise one's religion freely.

In 2006, Elaine Huguenin, a partner in a photography firm, was asked to photograph a commitment ceremony between two women. She refused, citing as a reason her biblically inspired belief that marriage is a union between a man and a woman. In arguments before the New Mexico Supreme Court, her attorneys invoked *Barnette* and *Wooley* in support of the principle that "the government may not compel people 'to engage in unwanted expression.'" Were Huguenin to lend her professional skills to the occasion, she would be expressing approval of it. But Justice Edward Chavez distinguished the case from *Barnette* and *Wooley* because, he said, they "involve situations in which the speakers were compelled to publicly 'speak the government's message.'" In contrast, the New Mexico Human Rights Commission (whose rules Huguenin was accused of violating) "does not require Elane Photography to recite or display any message." All it does is require "businesses that offer services to the public at large to provide those services without regard for race, sex, sexual orientation, or other protected classifications."[20] According to the court's logic, Huguenin is less compelled in her speech than the defendants in *Barnette* and *Wooley*. In *Barnette*, students had no choice but to attend public school and found themselves required to rehearse a patriotic affirmation with which they disagreed. Maynard could have chosen to let his automobile license expire, but had he done so in a rural state like New Hampshire, he would have rendered himself housebound. Elane Photography has more genuine choices, at least according to the New Mexico Supreme Court's opinion: it could have chosen to limit itself to a private clientele and not advertise to the general public, but once it did so advertise, it was bound by the laws governing public accommodations.

It could be argued, however, that Elane Photography's choice was no choice at all, but the exaction of a grievous price: if it wanted to be in business, it had to conform to the state's antidiscrimination laws, laws that prohibited making distinctions (like the distinction between marriage and same-sex cohabitation) to which the business's proprietors were religiously committed. In a concurrence, Justice Richard Bosson acknowledged that the Huguenins were being told by the law that they must "compromise the very religious beliefs that inspire their lives," but, he declared, that is "the price of citizenship." One could say that this means no more than that Elane Photography has to obey the law, and what could be wrong with that? What's wrong is that there is a Free Exercise Clause, which, if read strongly, prohibits state-imposed burdens on religious practice. If the clause is so read, the state is indeed unconstitutionally compelling Elaine Huguenin to affirm a message contrary to her faith, the message that the traditional definition of marriage is narrow and wrong and the new, enlarged definition of marriage announced in *Obergefell* is right. The court recognizes that this is a message "Elane Photography does not want to convey" but denies that it is in fact conveying it. It is the client who sends the message and owns it. Elane Photography merely provides the vehicle. That's what it is in business for, not to formulate or send messages but to offer a service (not unlike Western Union) for those who wish to do so: "It may be that Elane Photography expresses its clients' messages, but only because it is hired to do so." The hired hand, the court is saying, does the bidding of her employer; no one thinks that she originates or is the author of the employer's project, no more than anyone thinks that an actor is personally committed to the message of the lines she declaims.[21]

A second argument put forward by Elane Photography—that the New Mexico Human Rights Commission violated Huguenin's right to freely exercise her religion—fares no better. Only if the commission's regulations specifically and intentionally targeted religious activity—as the city of Hialeah, Florida, did when it wrote regulations designed to criminalize the practices of the Santería religion—could they be found in violation of the Free Exercise Clause.[22] That is not the situation here, said Justice Chavez. The act forbidding certain kinds of discrimination (but not all; it does not forbid discriminating against customers not wearing shoes) is neutral; the curtailing of religious practices was not its aim, although some religious practices may be caught up in its wake. If that happens, the fact that they have been restricted is just a side effect of a law that did not have that as its intention. (Remember Locke, Meliboeus, and the law forbidding animal slaughter: it was done for political, not religious reasons.) Justice Chavez cited

of Elane Photography made the same claim about taking pictures) and that it was his intention and desire to "honor God through his artistic talents," an intention that would be frustrated were he forced to create cakes for same-sex marriages. His speech would be compelled.

No, said the Colorado Court of Appeals. Phillips's cake-making may be artistic expression, but does it express the "particularized" message that same-sex marriage is to be celebrated? What is the likelihood "that a reasonable observer would both understand the message and attribute that message to Masterpiece?" Not very high, was the court's answer. "Rather, we conclude that a reasonable observer would understand that Masterpiece's compliance with the law is not a reflection of its own beliefs," for the sale of a cake to a same-sex couple "does not necessarily lead an observer to conclude that the baker supports its customer's conduct." All that can be concluded is that Masterpiece is in the business of producing and selling goods to the public and must abide by the laws governing commercial transactions.

So much for the compelled speech claim. And the free exercise claim? Masterpiece, like Elane Photography, tried to attach itself to *Church of Lukumi Babalu Aye v. City of Hialeah*, where the Supreme Court found a legislative intention to target a particular religion.[25] No such intention was found by the Colorado Court of Appeals: "[The Colorado Anti-Discrimination Act] does not compel Masterpiece to support or endorse any particular religious views." It "merely prohibits Masterpiece from discriminating against potential customers on account of their sexual orientation." Masterpiece, the court of appeals concluded, remains free to espouse its religious beliefs and to oppose same-sex marriage," but if "it wishes to . . . conduct business within the State of Colorado," it cannot pick and choose customers on the basis of their sexual orientation.

Together, *Elane Photography* and *Masterpiece* would seem to indicate a decisive victory (at least in the lower courts) for the rule of law and a defeat for a strong Free Exercise Clause that would allow believers to perform acts for which a nonbeliever would be penalized. But even before the Supreme Court agreed to hear *Masterpiece*, it gave some indication that the tide may be turning in the other direction. In *Hosanna-Tabor Evangelical Lutheran Church and School v. EEOC*, the Court strengthened the "ministerial exception," a doctrine that exempts churches from some generally applicable regulations, including regulations tied to antidiscrimination laws: while "the interest of society in the enforcement of employment discrimination statutes is undoubtedly important . . . so too is the interest of religious groups in choosing who will preach their beliefs, teach their faith, and carry out their mission."[26] The *Hosanna-Tabor* Court asserted that the second interest outweighs the first. And in *Burwell v. Hobby Lobby* the Court ruled in favor of a family corporation whose owners declined to comply with a regulation requiring them to provide contraceptives through health insurance to their employees; the owners argued that their religious beliefs count it as a sin against God "to be involved in the termination of human life."[27] So in these cases (and there are others) free exercise rights trump generally applicable laws.

It was thought that clarity might be achieved when the Supreme Court took up the *Masterpiece* case. But an exchange in oral arguments between Justice Sonia Sotomayor and Kristen Waggoner, a lawyer representing Jack Phillips, revealed a divide no opinion could bridge. Sotomayor said, "You can choose to sell cupcakes or not, whatever it is you choose to sell, you have to sell it to everyone who knocks on your door." (She privileges the requirement of equality before the law.) Waggoner replied, "I think that the gravest offense to the First Amendment would be to compel a person who believes that marriage is sacred to give voice to a different view of marriage, and require them to celebrate that marriage." (She privileges the free exercise of religion.) Sotomayor retorted, "Then don't participate in weddings." Waggoner had the last word, but it was the same word she spoke before: "A wedding cake expresses an inherent message that is that the union is a marriage and is to be celebrated and that message violates Mr. Phillips's religious convictions."

Obviously, this back-and-forth could have gone on forever without anyone giving an inch because Sotomayor and Waggoner were speaking from radically different initial positions: Sotomayor from a belief that generally applicable laws cannot bend to religious convictions without creating a government of men, not laws (a government where religious believers get to decide which regulations they will honor); and Waggoner a belief that the Free Exercise Clause prohibits the government from impeding the free exercise of religion, even when that exercise takes the form of words and acts the law forbids. Sotomayor and Waggoner live in different legal universes.

So it is not surprising that little was settled when the Court ruled on June 4, 2018. The ruling favored Phillips, but for a reason that left the underlying issues unresolved. Noting that during the hearing conducted by the Colorado Civil Rights Commission at least one member of the commission was dismissive of religious views and declared them responsible for atrocities like slavery and the Holocaust, Justice Kennedy, writing for the majority, argued that Phillips had been denied "the neutral and respectful consideration of his claims" in a manner that "cast doubt on the fairness and impartiality of the Commission's adjudication."[28] (In dissent, Justice Ruth Bader Ginsburg wondered how a few remarks during a commission hearing could "infect" a process that "involved several layers of independent decisionmaking of which the Commission was but one.") Left unanswered by Kennedy is the question of what will happen when a case posing the same issue but unburdened by any apparent hostility to religion reaches the Court, as it surely will. Perhaps then there will be a direct and clean reconsideration of "the delicate question of when the free exercise of . . . religion must yield to an otherwise valid exercise of state power."

That reconsideration, starring the same cast of characters, may be on the horizon. On the very day the Supreme Court delivered its narrow opinion, Jack Phillips was asked by a lawyer, Autumn Scardina, to create a cake with a blue exterior and a pink interior, a design that signified, she said, her transgender status. Phillips refused on the familiar grounds that the message was one his religion opposes. Within a few weeks the Colorado Civil Rights Division found him in violation of a Colorado antidiscrimination statute. On cue, the Alliance Defending Freedom brought a cause of action, *Masterpiece Cakeshop v. Elenis*, alleging that Phillips's free exercise rights had been infringed. The first signatory to the filing of the new case was Kristin Waggoner, the same lawyer who jousted with Justice Sotomayor in the *Masterpiece* oral arguments. In March 2019, Jack Phillips and the State of Colorado announced that they had "mutually agreed to end their ongoing state and federal court litigation." Both sides issued statements indicating that whatever settlement had been reached, it was not the end of the matter. The Alliance Defending Freedom declared that the settlement agreement was "a victory for Jack Phillips." Daniel Ramos, executive director of One Colorado, a gay and lesbian advocacy group, insisted in a statement that despite the settlement agreement, "the law is still the law." Coloradans, he declared, "are still protected . . . from discrimination in the areas of employment." Colorado's attorney general Phil Weiser acknowledged that "the larger constitutional issues might well be decided down the road." The odds are that *Masterpiece 2* will someday be playing in a courtroom near you.[29]

Get Out of My Restaurant!

Meanwhile, in a kind of sideshow, the question at the heart of both *Masterpiece* cases—*Under what circumstance can a merchant legally refuse service and say no to a customer?*—made it into the news again when on June 23, 2018, Sarah Huckabee Sanders, then press secretary to President Trump, was asked to leave the Red Hen restaurant in Lexington, Virginia, a picture-perfect southern town, home to Washington and Lee University. The restaurant's owner, Stephanie Wilkinson, explained that she did what she did because in her view Huckabee Sanders works for an "inhumane and unethical" administration. Almost immediately the parallel between this incident and Jack Phillips's unwillingness to create and bake a cake for a gay couple's wedding was drawn, and many on the conservative side pointed out that in all likelihood those who applauded the refusal of service at the Red Hen had earlier condemned the refusal of service in the bakery. The cry of "double standard" was heard in the land.

Actually the parallel is not all that exact. Phillips turned away Craig and Mullins because he did not wish to lend his skill to a union his religion condemned, and in so doing he discriminated against a class protected by the Colorado Anti-Discrimination Act. Wilkinson turned away a customer because she disapproved of her politics, and antidiscrimination laws do not, except in a few precincts, list as a protected class those who hold and express political views. Therefore the fate of Wilkinson's business will be in the hands not of the courts but of her neighbors in Lexington.

But even if this incident is somewhat off to the side of the questions raised by *Masterpiece*, it does touch on the more general question of whether someone who offers wares to the public should withhold them from people she dislikes, whether or not it is legal to do so. On that question, Wilkinson's case seems weak. She said to Huckabee Sanders that her restaurant "has certain standards that [she] feel[s] it has to uphold, such as honesty, and compassion and cooperation."[30] But any standards the restaurant upholds are standards that must be met by its proprietor and her employees, not by the customers. Wilkinson's obligation is to be honest in her dealings with her clientele by charging fair prices and providing quality ingredients. Presumably compassion comes in when she gives an employee who messed up a second chance or calls a cab for an inebriated customer rather than just throwing him out. On their part, the restaurant's customers should comport themselves civilly, not be disruptive, treat staff courteously, and pay promptly. Any other demand made on them, like the demand that they hold certain political beliefs, would seem to suggest that a restaurant has the right to monitor not only the behavior of customers when they *are* customers but the behavior they evidence as parents or voters or neighbors or grocery-store shoppers or Little League coaches and on and on. It's hard to see any basis for that right, which, if granted, would make a small restaurant you visit once or twice a year the arbiter of everything you think and do.

Some of those on Wilkinson's side pointed to Huckabee Sanders's celebrity status as a justification for asking her to leave. She's not just a diner with political views; she's a diner whose political views are known to everyone who has a computer or a cell phone or a TV; allowing her to remain would send a message that her views (actually Trump's views) are being endorsed by the restaurant. But serving Huckabee Sanders would signify only that she had a reservation, was properly dressed, and behaved herself, just as the fact that she chose to come to this restaurant signified no more than her judgment (now unhappily overturned) that she was going to enjoy a good meal. No one could reasonably think that by patronizing the restaurant Huckabee Sanders signed on to the politics of its owner and staff, and no one could reasonably think that by seating her the restaurant put the seal of its approval on the Trump administration.

Secularizing Religion in the Name of Pluralism

So in the end the Huckabee Sanders–Red Hen saga has little relevance to the issue left hanging in *Masterpiece*. That issue, as I've said, remains open and will always remain open even if it is decided differently next year or the year after. For should a later decision go the other way (in favor of generally applicable laws and against strong free exercise), it will mark only a temporary swing of the pendulum. The swinging cannot be arrested by a formula because the opposing positions issue from incompatible world views that cannot move toward each other in a spirit of compromise. You can't split this baby, although there is an army of legal academics trying to do just that. Typically their strategy (a version of the strategy employed to launder the religion out of religious symbols) is to deny the distinctiveness of religion and subsume it in a larger category that includes secular activities. This is the pluralist move: religion is protected (at least in part) not because of what it is but because of what it is like. For political theorist Cécile Laborde, the larger category under which religion is subsumed includes practices that are "expressive of *individual integrity*."[31] Religion is surely one of these, but so are other "life projects" (her term) citizens pursue: a dedication to environmental health, an all-consuming resolution to minister to the poor, a determination to root out political corruption, any passion in relationship to which one says "This is who I am." It is more than possible that a zealous commitment to a social or moral goal that is not religious in the usual sense will generate behavior that runs up against a generally applicable law;

when that happens, Laborde explains, there must be a formula that recognizes the centrality of the practice to those who engage in it while taking into account the harms and costs suffered by those for whom the practice is not central or even significant.

Here is her proposed formula: When a commitment of the kind that involves what she calls a deep "identity claim" is burdened by existing law, four questions should be asked. "1. How direct is the burden? 2. How severe is the burden? 3. How proportionate is it to the aim pursued by the law? 4. Can it be alleviated without excessive cost shifting?" Laborde asks, first, whether the burden a law places on free exercise is so great that an accommodation seems reasonable, and, second, whether allowing the accommodation leaves intact the core purpose of the law whose restrictions are being relaxed. Her questions assume (a) that the issue is one of balance, and (b) that the balance (or proportion) is a measure all parties do or should accept. No acknowledgment, except for an implicitly negative one, is made of those who might reject a balance because as a standard it supplants the faith-based standard to which they are committed. By assuming that balance is an obviously good thing, Laborde sidesteps and stigmatizes the often uncompromising nature of religious obligation. Her reasoning is clear and, from the perspective of liberal pluralism, persuasive: in a society where cooperation among citizens endowed with equal rights is the goal—everyone should have some room to live the life he or she chooses, but no one should occupy so much space that others lead lives that are pinched—there must be limits on "the untrammeled pursuit of people's life projects." Were there no limits, Laborde explains, there would be no "fair framework for the sharing of the burdens and benefits in common." So give a little, get a little, compromise, and be mindful of the other fellow's life plans.

That sounds more than reasonable if fairness is a central word in your vocabulary, as it is for those pluralists who see no essential difference between religion and other "life projects." But fairness—equal treatment of everyone in the relevant population—is not what strong religious believers are after. They are in possession of, and possessed by, a truth, and they want to testify to it at all times and in all contexts. They will not respond positively when Laborde insists that "all religious believers must take some responsibility for the pursuit of their integrity-protecting practices out of consideration for the fair pursuit of other citizens' projects and opportunities." That consideration will move them only if, for some unfathomable reason, they have set aside their religious beliefs and installed in their place a belief in fairness, equal respect, and the other virtues that are liberalism's content, if, in Laborde's words, they have signed on to a "higher-order interest in living under political justice on this earth . . . rather than in living by the word of God."

But why on earth would they do that? What makes the maintenance of the civil community an interest higher than the interest—obeying God's will—that is, in their view, really higher? (I am not suggesting that religious believers have no regard for fairness and equal respect, only that they do not worship them.) Why should Kim Davis care that couples she refuses to serve are forced to go elsewhere, suffering both shame and inconvenience? Why should Jack Phillips care that those he will not bake for must search for another baker, perhaps in another town? Indeed, if these would-be participants in a sinful practice are discomforted and blocked (for a while) from completing their "project," so much the better for *them*. At least for a few hours or days they will have been saved (despite themselves) from doing something that will harm their immortal souls. What Laborde and other liberal theorists fail to do is confront religion's claim to have a special purchase on the truth; or rather, they confront it either by ridiculing it as a claim a liberal state cannot take seriously (that, in fact, is right) or by removing it from the picture when they bundle religious speech with other discourses that articulate a "particular conception of the good." In this way, Laborde explains, the state "respects and protects religion, but only as one of the ways in which citizens live a life they think good." What this means, as Timothy Garton Ash explains, is that while the state must exhibit respect for the believer as believer, it needn't and shouldn't extend that respect to what the believers believe, especially when their beliefs lead to acts of discrimination the state forbids. Garton Ash sees the difficulty (a mild word) this makes for believers: "How can it be right to accept what is wrong?"[32] The answer, he says (it is Laborde's answer too), is that the believer's sense of right must give way to "a higher good," higher, that is, than the good named by his religion, which has now become a secondary aspect of his being, something to be "respected," but not something to be taken seriously.

At the same time that Laborde, Garton Ash, and other liberal theorists labor to deny religion the distinctiveness it claims, that same distinctiveness has been recognized by decisions like *Hosanna-Tabor* that honor the "ministerial exception" and allow religious associations to discriminate in ways that would be legally culpable if those engaging in the discrimination were not attached to a faith-based tradition. Law professors Ira C. Lupu and Robert W. Tuttle ask whether "other nonprofit organizations, like the Red Cross . . . could plausibly make similar claims of exemption from anti-discrimination laws."[33] It would, they say, be "unthinkable that our courts would be even remotely sympathetic to such assertions." Why unthinkable? Because the asserted exemption could not be justified by its source in a form of life that the state is barred from regulating and incapable of understanding. Religion, Lupu and Tuttle state flatly, "is constitutionally distinctive and cannot be fully subsumed within more general ideas of legal doctrines." Subsuming religion within a more general category is what pluralist theorists like Laborde are forever trying to do, but their efforts will always founder on the rock of religion's unwillingness to share the field of authority. "Religious practice and doctrine tends to be marked by the comprehensiveness and ultimacy of the claims made on adherents," claims that "transcend . . . all other loyalties, political, social, or familial." Accordingly, no reason or set of reasons can stand against the reason—derided by liberal commentators—that my religion compels me to do it or my religion forbids me to do it. That is the reasoning the liberal state cannot take seriously; in the pinch, Laborde declares, "[c]itizenship trumps religious commitment."[34] This is an assertion no deeply religious person can accept, for as law professors Susanna Mancini and Michel Rosenfeld explain, "from the standpoint of strong or fundamentalist religions, there are no legitimate means to weigh any secular interest against any categorical divine command."[35] It is from the standpoint of "strong or fundamentalist religions" that I have considered the issues explored in this chapter. It is the faithful members of those religions in the act of refusing to compromise their commitments who command my attention because they pose the relevant issues so sharply. To be sure, there are many sincerely religious persons who do not experience this conflict as deeply as a Kim Davis or a Jack Phillips, but the position taken by Davis, Phillips, and their compatriots is the one that is more interesting because it lays bare the deepest questions.

I can imagine some readers (on liberalism's side) resisting the implication that a concern for the salvation of souls might override the secular obligation to treat all—sinners, saints, backsliders, blasphemers—equally, an obligation Davis arguably took on when she became county clerk, and an obligation Phillips might be thought to have assumed when he opened his doors to the public. Putting it that way shows (once again) the gulf that separates the opposing parties in these disputes. It is a battle between those for whom obedience to the will of a transcendent God is primary and those who regard talk of a transcendent God as childish prattle that we are required by the Constitution to allow but are encouraged by the same Constitution to marginalize, at least for the purposes of law and government. Those who regard religious belief as a quaint relic of medieval ignorance will allow believers to order their personal lives by their faith: if they make decisions because they think God is speaking to them, they must be permitted to do so; that's the tolerance of the liberal state. But should they want their private revelations to be written into law, they will be out of luck in the same liberal state whose tolerance does not extend to sharing the political franchise with a rival. As Robert Post, a liberal theorist of the first order, explains, "[H]owever much society may respect the integrity of personal beliefs, claims for conscientious exemptions must at some point be denied." While the "faithful can continue politics by becoming gadflies, they cannot require law to undermine itself."[36]

The First Amendment as a Religion: The Battle of the Two Faiths

In the previous paragraphs I have been ventriloquizing the voices of the various parties to these disputes, adopting alternately the tone and the vocabulary of each of the opposing combatants. I did that to indicate that I am not taking a side but illustrating why the two sides are irreconcilable. And at the heart of that irreconcilability is the insight with which I began this chapter: the Religion Clause, and especially the Free Exercise Clause, is an anomaly; it doesn't belong, for it opens a door—the door to theocratic influence, even dominance—the rest of the Constitution closes shut. It is tempting to describe the struggle as one between theological fiat and rational common sense (and that is certainly how "new atheists" Richard Dawkins, Sam Harris, and Christopher Hitchens describe it), but it would be more accurate to frame it as a struggle between two different theologies.[37] Given the basic and inviolable assumptions underlying the two positions, the propositions that issue from each are entirely rational, at least from that perspective. And to the extent that each position is a creed rooted in an unchallengeable conviction—either the conviction that true authority transcends mortal norms and measures or the conviction that mortal norms and measures are all we have—each position is a theology.

The tendency in some quarters to regard the First Amendment as an object of worship (it trumps everything) is on display in a number of Supreme Court decisions where the bare assertion of a speech interest is a sufficient counterweight to the harms caused by its exercise. One clear example is *Snyder v. Phelps*, the case (referenced in chapter 2) in which the Court by an 8–1 vote held for the Westboro Baptist Church, notorious for intruding on the funerals of young soldiers by waving signs saying "Thank God for dead soldiers" and "You're going to Hell."[38] The church is motivated by the belief that God disapproves of the tolerance increasingly extended to gays and lesbians in this country and is expressing his disapproval through the death of these soldiers (who are not presumed by the church to be gay). In dissent, Justice Samuel Alito wondered why "the nation's commitment to free and open debate" should be a license for "vicious verbal assault." Chief Justice Roberts, writing for the majority, acknowledged the great pain inflicted on the parents of young men who died serving their country, but declared that nevertheless "[w]e cannot react to the pain by punishing the speaker. As a nation we have chosen a different course—to protect even hurtful speech on public issues." (The public issue here is the moral status of homosexuals.) Roberts here rejects any balancing of First Amendment rights against the evils they might on occasion produce. In an earlier case, *United States v. Stevens*, Roberts made his position explicit: the First Amendment "reflects a judgment by the American people that the benefits of its restrictions . . . outweigh the costs."[39] If the First Amendment is placed on one scale, no amount of harms piled up on another can outweigh it.

In *Stevens* the costs include the kittens that are crushed to death by the spiked shoes of a dominatrix in the videos whose legality the Court affirms. (To be precise, it is the legality of the representation, not of the act represented, that is affirmed; killing cats in that manner is animal cruelty; filming the killing is not.) In the famous (or notorious) *Citizens United v. Federal Election Commission* decision, the cost is the possible and likely corruption that would follow if restrictions on campaign expenditures were relaxed.[40] The arguments of both the majority and the dissenters are detailed and complicated and speak to whether a corporation is a person and whether the old proverb "Money talks" can be translated into First Amendment doctrine. But for Justice Kennedy one fact trumps everything else: "Section 441b's prohibition on corporate independent expenditures is . . . a ban on speech." Game over! Any regulation that restricts the flow of free speech is per se invalid. There's nothing more to say, although both sides go on to say a great deal.

These three decisions (and there are others) exhibit the characteristics of a theology, one of whose features is that it does not distinguish between minor and major departures from core tenets; any departure is seen as a breach in a wall that must be maintained intact. That is precisely the stance of strong First Amendment adherents when they are urged to relax the severity of their position in the face of documented harms; they are being asked to turn their back on their faith and, understandably, they recoil from such a request. When publishers in this country and elsewhere gratuitously reprinted the infamous "Danish cartoons" regarded by many Muslims as an assault on their religion, they did so, they testified, not because the cartoons were news or because editors were hostile to Islam, but because they wished to stand up for their own religion, the religion of free speech.[41] Timothy Garton Ash, a member in good standing of the Church of Free Speech, tried, in response to the attack on the magazine *Charlie Hebdo* in 2015, to launch "an appeal for a week of solidarity in which a wide range of newspapers would simultaneously publish a selection of the *Charlie Hebdo* cartoons with an explanation of why they were doing so."[42] Presumably, the explanation would have nothing to do with the issues raised by the cartoons but with the obligation, in effect a religious obligation, to publish them as evidence of doctrinal fidelity. Garton Ash was asking good free-speech liberals to stand up for their faith.

Since the beginning of this chapter, I have spoken of the Religion Clause as an anomaly; perhaps it would be more accurate to say that it represents the unacknowledged intrusion into one religious discourse of the imperatives and claims of another. It is as if the first of the amendments to a Constitution inspired by liberalism's faith announces a principle—*Religious speech is special*—that belongs to a rival faith. Liberalism's faith rests on a belief in the free choice of autonomous individuals not bound by preexisting authority or by the edicts that authority issues. Religion's faith rests on a system of belief grounded in a transcendent being whose commands we must obey. It is hardly surprising that this ill fit between the Constitution as a whole and one prominent part of it that breathes a different spirit generates a body of cases that cannot be reconciled within some rule or principle.

Indeed, it's worse than that, for the Religion Clause is itself fissured by its two subclauses, one elevating religious speech to a position of privilege, the other warning against religious speech as the potential portal of theocracy. To say that these two clauses pull against each other is an understatement. And indeed it is even worse than *that*. Both the Free Exercise Clause and the Establishment Clause have strong and weak versions. The Free Exercise Clause has been read as doing nothing more than glossing the Free Expression Clause: you can't be stopped from having religious thoughts or declaring them. But the Free Exercise Clause has also been read as legitimating religiously inspired acts even when they are in violation of generally applicable laws. In the same double way, the Establishment Clause has been read generously as accommodating religious speech in the public sphere as long as the accommodation doesn't amount to an outright establishment (no Church of America), and it has been read severely as forbidding any commerce at all between religion and the civil state in the spirit of James Madison's insistence in his "Memorial and Remonstrance" (1785) that not "three pence" of public funds be directed to religious institutions.

So we have a contradiction within an anomaly, and within the contradiction a set of opposing definitions, all combining to fashion a jurisprudence that is unstable, vertiginous, and often just plain crazy. That jurisprudence, like First Amendment jurisprudence in general, is in search of a principle, but what it finds and participates in is the endless alternation between the competing requirements of liberal egalitarian theory and fidelity to religious doctrine. Neither requirement will ever command the field unless either the Religion Clause is repealed or the country becomes a theocracy.

And where do I stand? On the substantive questions raised in this chapter, I could go either way. I'm fine with allowing religious monuments in public spaces. I'm fine with insisting that the public sphere be religion-free. I'm fine with letting a few bakers refuse to create cakes for same-sex weddings. I'm fine with enforcing antidiscrimination laws strictly and forcing the bakers to comply. What both amuses and vexes me are the acrobatics performed by those who are assigned the task of applying a piece of the Constitution at odds with its informing spirit, those who get around the Establishment Clause by declaring, in the face of all the evidence, that religious monuments and symbols are not religious, and those who claim to honor religious-free exercise but restrict exercise to practices cut off from religion's central claim to be preeminently authoritative. Of course, by my own argument, these acrobatics should not be the occasion for criticism because those who perform them have been forced to do so by the anomalies and contradictions that will always frustrate their efforts to make constitutional sense.

Titsworth reported that the group's first action was to affirm transparency as one of its "core values"; its second action was to decide unanimously that its meetings would be held in private. As you can imagine, it was easy to make fun of the obvious contradiction, but the contradiction is not so glaring once we understand that two notions of what "free" means are in play here. The group wants (understandably) to be free of the pressures that would be felt if the proceedings were conducted under public scrutiny: at every moment members would be tempted to tailor what they said to the responses and criticisms of an imagined audience. In short, they would not be speaking freely but under a shadow if the meaning of "freely" in force were "entirely without filters, gatekeepers, and boundaries." *That* sense of freely is championed by techno-utopians whose mantra is "Information wants to be free" and who believe that the glorious future predicted by the authors of every technological advance—a future in which democracy's potential is finally realized in a communication community where everyone is heard and no one is marginalized—is just around the corner: no one hoarding information or controlling access or deciding who speaks and who doesn't. What Titsworth and his fellow committee members see is that this more ambitious and abstract sense of "free" is antithetical to the successful completion of their task. Not speaking freely in front of everyone is a condition of speaking freely—without anxiety and mental reservation—on the way to exploring the complexities and difficulties of their charge. As law professor David Pozen explains, open-meeting laws have "been found to chill candor, hamper compromise, [and] shift deliberation into backroom channels."[1] At the beginning of the republic, James Madison explained that had the Constitutional Convention pledged itself to transparency, members would have felt pressure to maintain whatever views they first expressed, whereas in a closed, secret discussion "no man felt himself obliged to retain his opinions any longer than he was satisfied of their propriety and truth."[2] Madison's point is that the emergence of truth is *less* likely if transparency is enforced.

The moral is that transparency is not an unambiguously good thing. (I pass over for the moment the prior and deeper question of whether it is a possible thing.) And if that is right, then the proliferation of speech may not be a good thing either; silence and the withholding of speech may be useful and even necessary in some contexts, such as the context of preparing a report or the context of a marriage or the context of implementing a foreign policy. I am aware that many free-speech advocates believe that the more free speech there is, the better the human condition will be, and believe too that it is the business of our institutions, including our legislatures and courts, to increase the amount of speech available. In its decisions, the Supreme Court more than occasionally favors the alternative that adds to the speech citizens regularly receive.

At first glance the bias in favor of unlimited speech and information seems perfectly reasonable and even unassailable. What arguments could be brought against it? An answer to that question has been offered in recent years by a small, but growing, number of critics. In 2009, law professor Lawrence Lessig, known as an apostle of openness, began an essay with the title "Against Transparency" by asking, as I just have, "How could anyone be against transparency?"[3] Lessig responds to his own question by quoting a trio of authors who, in their book *Full Disclosure: The Perils and Promise of Transparency*, observe that by itself information doesn't do anything; its effects depend on the motives of those who make use of it; raw information cannot distinguish between benign and malign appropriations of itself: "[R]esponses to information are inseparable from . . . interests, desires, resources, cognitive capacities and social contexts." Misunderstanding and manipulation are always more than possible—indeed their possibility increases with increases in the amount of information—and there is no way to assure that "new information is used to further public objectives" rather than the objectives of some partisan or even criminal agenda.[4] There may be situations, Lessig acknowledges, when transparency facilitates rational choosing (his example is the requirement that car manufacturers publish average miles-per-gallon statistics), but in other situations transparency—living every moment of our lives in the light celebrated by Brandeis when he declared that sunlight is "the best of disinfectants"—can bring with it inefficiency, misjudgments, premature conclusions, and ruined careers. Infatuated as we are by the "unquestioned goodness" of transparency, "we are not," Lessig warns, "thinking critically enough about where and when transparency works, and where and when it may lead to confusion, or to worse."

Another way to put this is to say that information, data, and the unbounded flow of speech—supposedly the antithesis of political manipulation—can be woven into a narrative that constricts rather than expands the area of free, rational choice. Transparency and the unbounded flow of speech can be instruments in the production of the very inequalities (economic, political, educational) the gospel of openness promises to remove. And the more this gospel is preached and believed—the more the answer to everything is assumed to be data uncorrupted by interests and motives—the easier it will be for interests and motives to operate under transparency's cover. Internet prophets will fail to see the political dangers of openness because they believe that it is politics they are removing by delivering data in its raw—not selectively arranged—form. In this utopian vision, faction and difference—the twin motors of politics—will just wither away when the defect that generates them, the defect of distorted communication, has been eliminated by unmodified data circulated freely between free and equal consumers; everyone will be on the same page, reading from the same script, and apprehending the same *universal*—shared by all instantaneously—meaning. Back to Eden!

The internet critic Evgeny Morozov describes and mocks the dream: "If today's blogs, wikis, and social networks allow instantaneous and infinite deliberations, if they allow us to replace leadership [i.e., monitoring guardians] . . . and get rid of bureaucracy in its entirety, why bother with the old system at all?"[5] Why bother, that is, with congresspersons, presidents, political parties, administrative agencies, elites, judges, universities, experts, public intellectuals—all the persons, structures, and institutions that intervene between us and unmediated, transparent fact. Agreement and harmony will just emerge by virtue of an electronic lingua franca.

This utopian fantasy rests on a perfectionist view of human nature: rather than being doomed by original sin to conflict, prejudice, and the will to power, men and women are by nature communitarian, inclined to fellowship and the seeking of common ground. However, the story continues, these good instincts have been blocked by language differences that can now be transcended by the digital revolution. Facebook's Mark Zuckerberg once said of Middle East animosities that they do not have a source in "deep hatred" (who knew?) but instead stem "from the lack of connectedness and lack of communication."[6] Zuckerberg, says Morozov, "believes that if only we were all connected, if only Facebook were available everywhere and everyone had an account, all misunderstanding would cease and all wars would stop." Here is a Facebook press release that makes explicit the claim and the hope: "By enabling people from diverse backgrounds to easily connect and share their ideas, we can decrease world conflict in the short and long run." Difference, the source of dissension leading to war, will be eliminated by the universal solvent of data. Talk about magical thinking!

In the alternative (and I believe true) story, human difference is irreducible, and there is no "neutral observation language" (a term of Thomas Kuhn's in his 1962 book *The Structure of Scientific Revolutions*) that can bridge, soften, blur, and perhaps eventually erase the differences that separate us and put us at odds. There are only vocabularies attached to particular practices and constituencies, vocabularies whose meanings derive from those practices, meanings that are local, shared by members of these constituencies and opaque to outsiders. When persons from different constituencies clash, there is no common language to which they can refer their differences for mechanical resolution; there are only political negotiations (and if those fail, war), the content of which is not truth-telling—although truths are occasionally told—but propaganda, threats, insults, deceptions, exaggerations, insinuations, bluffs, posturings, in short all the forms of verbal manipulation that were supposedly to have disappeared in the internet nirvana.

They won't. Indeed they will proliferate because the politically angled speech that is supposedly the source of our problems is in fact the only possible route to their (no doubt temporary) solution. Speech proceeding from a point of view can at least be recognized as such and then countered. You can say, "I know where those guys are coming from, and here are my reasons for believing that we should be coming from somewhere else"; dialogue then begins—no doubt dialogue inflected by interests and agendas, but dialogue still. But when speech (or information or data) is just sitting there unattached to any perspective but floating freely in the frictionless air, when there are no guidelines, monitors, gatekeepers, or filters, what you have are innumerable Lego-like bits available for assimilation into any project a clever verbal engineer might imagine. What you don't have is any mechanism that can stop the construction project or even assess it. What you have, in short, are the perfect conditions for the unchecked proliferation of what has come to be called "fake news." Those are the same conditions, along with the hope that they will by themselves deliver truth, that we met in the earlier discussion of the Marketplace of Ideas. The unregulated "free" internet and the radically open marketplace are one and the same: they promise liberation but yield confusion and bondage.

Fake News and Postmodernism

Now I know that the rise of fake news has been attributed by some to the emergence of postmodern thought, which, says Victor Davis Hanson, a scholar at the Hoover Institution in Palo Alto, "derides facts and absolutes and insists that there are only narratives and interpretations."[7] That's not quite right. The insistence on the primacy of narratives and interpretations does not involve a deriding of facts but an alternative account of their emergence. Postmodernism sets itself against the notion of facts just lying there, discrete and independent and waiting to be described. Facts, it tells us, don't preexist interpretation and argument; facts emerge in the course of interpretation and argument. Fact is not a preexisting entity by whose measure argument can be assessed. Arguments come first; when they are successful, facts follow, at least for a while, until a new round of arguments replaces them with a new set of facts. This is far from the picture of interpretive nihilism Hanson and other anti-postmodernists paint. One cannot simply declare facts as an act of the unbridled will and assume they will stick; one must work though the protocols of argument present in any well-developed practice. Someone who has negotiated these protocols in a way that is persuasive to his or her fellows will have participated in the establishment of fact. Friction, not free invention, is the heart of this process: you commit yourself to the standards of evidence long in place in the conversation you enter, and then you maneuver as best you can within the guidelines of those standards. A judge who issues a decision cannot simply decide which side she favors and then deliver an opinion. Even if she has a firm idea of where she wants to go from the beginning, she must pass through the authorized routes for getting there; sometimes she will fail and say that, despite her interpretive desires, "this opinion just won't write."

Any opinion will write if there are no routes to be negotiated or standards to hew to, if your interpretive desires meet no obstacles when you wish to assemble or reassemble bits of unmoored data into a story that serves your purposes. It is not postmodernism that licenses this irresponsibility but the doctrine that freedom of information and transparency are all we need. Those who proclaim this theology—and theology it is—can in good faith bypass all the usual routes of validation because their religion tells them that those routes are corrupt and that only the nonmethod of having no routes, no boundaries, no categories, no silos can bring us to the River Jordan and beyond. In many versions of Protestantism, parishioners are urged to reject merely human authority in any form and go directly to the pure Word of God. For present-day technophiles the pure Word is to be found in unfiltered data. In fact, however, what is found in a landscape where unattached data proliferate without context or constraint is the fracturing of the Word into innumerable pieces of disjointed information, all existing side by side, indifferently approved, and no way of distinguishing between them, no way of telling which of them is true or at least has a claim to be true and which of them is made up out of whole cloth. De-authorizing traditional authoritative institutions—and that is what transparency advocates always promise—removes any possibility of making the distinctions that would lead one to say "This piece of news has a solid pedigree, and this piece of news doesn't." In the brave new world of transparency, every piece of data is its own pedigree and has as great a claim to your credulity as any other.

That is the world in which fake news flourishes. Fake news is created by the undermining of trust in the traditional vehicles of authority and legitimation: newspapers of record, professional associations, credentialed academics, standard encyclopedias, research libraries, authenticated archives, government bureaus, federal courts, prime-time news anchors. When Walter Cronkite was the longtime anchor at CBS, he was known as the most trusted man in America. When he signed off by saying "And that's the way it is," everyone believed him. It didn't matter whether every single thing he said in his broadcasts was true; what mattered was that his audience regarded him as someone dedicated to the reporting of truth and accepted him as a touchstone of trust. That trust could survive the occasional revelation of error. It could not survive a casual indifference to whether something said was backed up by reputable sources or backed up by nothing at all.

That corrosive indifference has been given its technical name by the philosopher Harry Frankfurt in the title of his famous little book, *On Bullshit*.[8] It's bullshit, Frankfurt explains, when the speaker "does not reject the authority of truth, as the liar does," but instead "pays no attention to it" because he just doesn't care. Unlike the liar, the bullshitter is not intent on obscuring the facts, for "his eye is not on the facts at all . . . except insofar as they may be pertinent to his intent in getting away with what he says." The bullshitter, Frankfurt concludes, is "a greater enemy of truth" than the liar, for while the liar mounts an assault on truth and displays a negative regard for it, the bullshitter appropriates truth when convenient and does less honor to it than its avowed enemy.

This indifference to the truth status of an utterance is a feature of the internet, where authority is evenly distributed to everyone with a voice or a podcast, and no one believes anybody, or (it is the same thing) everyone believes anybody. This wholesale distrust of authoritative mechanisms leads to the bizarre conclusion that an assertion of fact is more credible if it lacks an institutional source: if information comes from nowhere and is authorized by no one, it must be true. In this line of reasoning, a piece of news originating in a blog maintained by a teenager in a basement in Idaho would be more reliable than a piece of news announced by the anchor of a major network. What recommends the news anchor over the teenager is that the former feels a responsibility to the facts, while the latter—an internet bullshitter—does not. Feeling a responsibility to the facts does not mean that you get them right but that you are at least working to get them right. Real news is not news that corresponds to objective fact—that would be an impossible standard—but news delivered by those who *aspire* to that correspondence. Bullshitters have no such aspiration, and in the absence of gatekeepers they purvey their wares largely unimpeded by the checks and balances we have always relied on. And, again, what has brought us to this sorry pass are not the writings of Derrida or Foucault or any other postmodernist, but the twin mantras of "More free speech" and "Absolute transparency."

The Danger of Unbounded Information

Nowhere has the promise of transparency been more heralded than in the world of government reform. The idea is that if the government did its business out in the open, deception and corruption would be easily detected and honesty and efficiency would flourish. (It is this idea that impels the dishonest-but-presented-as-virtuous acts performed by Julian Assange, Edward Snowden, and Chelsea Manning.) But in his book *The Transparency Fix*, law professor Mark Fenster argues against the assumption that government information is something whose full revelation would result in the realization (with minimal political effort) of a true democracy.[9] No doubt, says Fenster, "this thing called government information exists," but so vast is its bulk, so heterogeneous are its documents, so multiple the categories into which it can be divided and subdivided that it cannot be digested or grasped: "It makes up a boundless archive that cannot be known." If it can't be known, nothing can be done with it; if "it" has no shape, it would be hard to come up with principles of selection that would make "it" manageable and operable; the more of it there is, the less is it of any use: "[T]he excess of available information limits the ability to know and understand any part of the state and its operation." In other words, the combination of transparency and the full flow of information leads not to enlightenment and clean government but to confusion and paralysis. That is why, as David Pozen explains, "[t]he 1970's reforms that opened up congressional committees and the House floor have yielded disappointment and dysfunction on a large scale."[10] There's just too much of the very stuff of which techno-utopians say there can't be too much. In a book aptly entitled *More Than You Wanted to Know*, law professors Omri Ben-Shahar and Carl E. Schneider identify the "overload problem": "Even willing minds can retain only a few things."[11] A mind inundated by data might think that it has "seen it all," but in fact the larger the amount of information, the more it will miss. We now live, law professor Tim Wu explains, in an age of "reverse censorship," when the flooding, not the suppression, of information makes it easy to drown out voices someone doesn't want heard. While traditional First Amendment law "presupposes an information-poor world" where speakers are "threatened by one terrible monster" (the censoring government), barriers to speaking have now been largely removed, and as a result speech is increasingly "cheap" and readily weaponized "to attack, harass they can fashion malevolent messages, secure in the knowledge that the gatekeeping norms that might expose and stop them are nowhere in sight because they have been discredited. That is why, Dreyfus concludes, the internet is a "perfect medium for slander and innuendo." Daniel J. Solove, writing on privacy law, explains, "[I]n the small village, people knew each other well, and disreputable information would be judged within the context of a person's entire life. Now, people are judged out of context based on information fragments found on line."[16] Brian Leiter offers the same judgment in harsher tones. He speaks of "cyber-cesspools" where vicious vituperation grows unchecked, and he formulates a sharp contrast between those who used to engage in traditional forums of deliberation and those "sociopaths" (his word) who delight in spewing venom and abuse on the net: "Prior to cyber-space, if you wanted to reach more than your immediate circle of acquaintances, you usually had to have some kind of competence, education, status, intelligence and ability. . . . [Y]ou generally had to be moderately sane. . . . [T]hat is no more." The journalist Matthew d'Ancona agrees: the internet, he says, has "enabled the worst of mankind's instincts, acting as a university for terrorists and a haven for con-men."[17]

Are Techno-Utopians Having Second Thoughts?

Internet enthusiasts tell a different story. They believe that more and more information will result in better and better choices by persons freed from the slanted perspectives offered by so-called expert authorities. Indeed it is even said that rational choosers emancipated from artificial constraints will become better persons. Recently, however, some tech entrepreneurs have expressed dismay and surprise when it turned out that what they had made available could be, and often was, turned to evil purposes. Facebook CEO Mark Zuckerberg acknowledged experiencing that surprise in his April 2018 testimony before Congress, and at moments seemed less sure than he had been about the internet's beneficial effects.[18] But when Republican senator Ben Sasse brought up the question of hate speech and asked what Facebook proposed to do about it, Zuckerberg expressed confidence that in time artificial intelligence would develop to the point where it would provide the necessary discriminations: "Hate speech—I am optimistic that over a five-to-ten year period we will have AI tools that can get into some of the linguistic nuances of different types of content . . . but today we're just not there." What Zuckerberg doesn't see, and doesn't want to see, is that we'll never be there. As historian Jerry Z. Muller explains in *The Tyranny of Metrics*, the big mistake of those who put their faith in quantitative methods—in the amassing and mining of data—is to think that they can model human judgment; they can't: "Practical or tacit knowledge is the product of experience: it can be learned, but cannot be conveyed in general formulas."[19] That is, it cannot be formalized, made into an algorithm.

After a driverless car killed a jaywalking pedestrian in the spring of 2018, machine-learning guru Andrew Ng blamed it on the failure of the victim to be sufficiently rule-governed.[20] Apparently the car's sensors had detected the jaywalker but discounted the data because they didn't fit into the computerized rules guiding the automobile. Those rules—the data-input into the sensors—are inflexible and presuppose agents who are inflexible too, agents who don't jaywalk and are programmed to do the rational and lawful thing. (Instead of "Why can't a woman be more like a man?," Ng's question is "Why can't a human be more like a machine?") But humans aren't like that; they are at once better and worse; they can adjust and improvise on the wing, something a driverless car can't do. Ng is in the grasp of what Muller calls the "rationalist illusion," the illusion that the imperfect, halting, contextual processes of human understanding can be improved by removing the "human factor" and turning the job over to numbers. As we saw in chapter 2, theorists have been trying for decades to do what Zuckerberg believes artificial intelligence will do in a few years: demarcate hate speech from speech in general. They have failed not because they didn't have an algorithm sophisticated enough to isolate the species, but because the entity they wished to pin down is protean and context-variable and hence incapable of being captured by patterns generated by a machine. While Zuckerberg hasn't yet figured that out, Yoon Lee, the head of product innovation at Samsung Electronics, has. Human thinking, he points out, is "malleable" and "gray," which means that "data should be used as more of an assistant" than as "the barometer for making the decision."[21] If you want to make good decisions, "instead of becoming an expert in data, you have to become an expert in that field and then try to understand the name of the game." Contextual knowledge first; judgment—aided, but not governed, by data—second. Brittan Heller, head of the Anti-Defamation League's Center for Technology and Study, responding to Zuckerberg's testimony, delivered the right lesson: "[E]ven the best of filters will not replace human reviewers."[22] Zuckerberg seems not to have learned anything; his techno-utopianism has not been muted or dampened but raised to a higher level.

Matthew Prince, the CEO of Cloudflare, a service that promises to "make the internet work for" its users without censoring anything, tells a more cautionary tale. To his distress (a distress that seems more genuine than Zuckerberg's) he found that Cloudflare had become the preferred home and protector of the Daily Stormer, a prominent neo-Nazi website. Cloudflare prided itself on being faithful to First Amendment principles and didn't want to set itself up as a censor even of messages it despised. (They're trying to be good First Amendment soldiers.) So when complaints about the Daily Stormer reached Cloudflare, the service sent them along with the complainants' contact information to the Daily Stormer in the hope that the complaint would be registered and routed to the proper place without compromising the First Amendment principle of open and equal access. But it turned out that those whose names had been passed on to the Daily Stormer "were getting harassing and threatening calls and emails."[23] Prince and his colleagues found themselves with a difficult choice: either they could remove the website and violate their First Amendment principles or let it stay up and be accused of having "ratted out decent people to an army of fascist trolls." "What we didn't antic-ipate," Prince said plaintively, "was that there are just truly awful human beings in the world." I would reword: what they didn't anticipate was that human beings are human beings informed by competing interests and not calculating devices.

Paul Berry, CEO of another social media service, said of Cloud-flare's dilemma, "[H]onestly I am so sad, I grew up in the Valley; I've been writing code since I was 10 and I believed in technology." Now he sees a tension between a viable social media service "and actually being human." Actually being human—taking sides and not relying on ever proliferating, unmonitored data to reveal the truth—won out when Prince kicked the Daily Stormer off the Cloudflare network and then flagellated himself in public for hav-ing done so. It would seem, as Tim Wu observes, "that celebrants of open and unfettered channels of internet expression (myself included) are being hoisted on their own petard."[24] Technology writer Kara Swisher expresses a similar chagrin in a *New York Times* piece with the headline "I Thought the Web Would Stop Hate, Not Spread It."[25]

Jack Dorsey, CEO of Twitter, traveled the same journey from techno-optimism to dismay at technology's unanticipated harmful effects. He said in a CNN interview that he and the other designers of the platform had not been alert "to the repercussions of [their] actions."[26] Once those repercussions appeared in the form of trolling, abuse, and misinformation (his words), he cast about for a fix, but the fixes he offered are little more than a collection of pieties. "Being a lot more open" is one, but being open is what got Twitter into trouble in the first place. "Provide more context" is another, but more context will only produce more opportunities for trolling, abuse, and misinformation. "Amplify the more credible sources" is a third, but that would involve Dorsey and his colleagues in determining what is and is not a credible source, and that is precisely what they don't want to do: "[I]t is dangerous for a company like ours to be an arbiter of truth." No doubt, but the dangers of *not* being an arbiter of truth—of being open—are what he is now dealing with as more and more criticism is leveled at his company for being a vehicle of deceit and propaganda. Like Zuckerberg and Prince, Dorsey faces a choice between acting as the gatekeeper of truth and thus incurring the wrath of open-information prophets, or letting everything in and incurring the wrath of those who hold him responsible for a polluted internet. Perhaps Zuckerberg, Dorsey, Berry, and Prince would have escaped tying themselves up in moral knots if, instead of reading John Perry Barlow's "A Declaration of the Independence of Cyberspace"[27]—a libertarian free-speech manifesto the author later backed away from when he discovered the need for regulation—they had read Cicero and Quintilian, from whom they would have learned that separating the real from the fake is the work not of piled-up raw data or of algorithms or of a perfected artificial intelligence, but of the arts of persuasion with which we build and later unbuild stories about what is true and what is not. Notice I say "build" and not "make up." These stories emerge not from our unfettered imaginations but from the traditions of sitting there all by itself and waiting to be discerned by clear-eyed observers. In this picture, which continues to be affirmed and celebrated in the popular imagination, truth exists prior to and independently of the efforts to specify it. In an alternative picture that has been with us since the Pre-Socratics, truth is created and manufactured, not in a pejorative sense but in the sense that it emerges in the course of deliberative inquiry that has been conducted within the protocols of evidence and argument in place in a particular practice.

In the "post-truther's" account of truth, "true" is a compliment paid to propositions that have been validated by a set of rules and procedures that are themselves contingent and revisable. Truth, writes sociologist Steve Fuller, is always "relative to the language in terms of which knowledge claims can be expressed."[28] When we say that something is true, we mean that it satisfies " 'truth conditions' as specified by the rules of a given language or practice, just as 'goal' corresponds to satisfying the rules of play in a given game." So, for example, a proposition offered by a historian is a candidate for being true if it has been arrived at by the routes of investigation and evidence-collecting authorized by the discipline of history; the archive can't be a collection of random data, and the evaluation of evidence must proceed according to criteria accepted as legitimate in the discipline. The same with the achieving of a goal in an athletic context. A player scores a goal in football if he is on the roster, is eligible to run or catch a pass, doesn't go out of bounds, and commits no fouls. There is, Fuller insists, no *general* sense either of truth or of goal that stands apart from their appearance in a particular man-made game presided over by that game's constitutive rules.

The game Fuller focuses on is science, thought by many to be not a game at all, but the location and engine of objective truth. Fuller challenges that characterization of science when he declares,

"What passes for the 'truth' in science is an institutionalized contingency which if scientists are doing their job will be eventually overturned and replaced." By "institutionalized contingency," Fuller means the norms and protocols that are in force not because Nature demands them but because by disciplinary and cultural routes that could have been otherwise (that's the contingency part), the scientific community (that's the institutionalized part) is persuaded, at least for a while, that *these* are the procedures which will lead us to the truth. This act of persuasion may "take" for a short time or for decades or even centuries, but it remains contingent; it can always be upended when researchers, for any number of reasons, many of them unpredictable, go down another path at the end of which they find a new truth. I hasten to add that revolutions in the characterization or description of the world do not change the world; what is true about the world remains true after accounts of what that truth is change. It is the accounts that are different, not the *Ding an sich* (the thing as it really is) the accounts aim at. That is what Thomas Kuhn means when he says in *The Structure of Scientific Revolutions* that "although the world does not change with a change of paradigm"—a change in the methods, evidentiary standards, and expectations with which we go about the business of attempting to circumscribe nature—"the scientist afterwards works in a different world." Ensconced in a new paradigm and armed with a new vocabulary that both enables and limits what can be described, scientists will see things they hadn't seen before and discount the reality of things they used to see. There is surely something out there not caused by our descriptions of it, but our descriptions of it provide us all the access to it that we can have. "No process yet disclosed by the historical study of scientific development resembles the methodological stereotype of falsification by nature."[29]

The scene of truth as described by Kuhn and Fuller is marked by revolutions: long-established and trusted traditions of inquiry can be exploded in a moment, for it is always possible that someone let into the game could turn it in a new and wholly unanticipated direction. But as Fuller observes, the very institutionalization of those traditions renders them resistant to challenges from the outside and leads them to have a decidedly conservative aspect; insiders want to memorialize and protect their achievement. What is being protected, often fiercely (witness the opposition by mainstream science to the theory of intelligent design), are not truth and fact per se but truth and fact as they have been established by disciplinary workers who, by virtue of their success in persuading the relevant community, occupy the position of authoritative elites and don't want to give it up. The efforts by credentialed practitioners to hold on to their monopoly of intellectual and cultural authority can be said to have its good side: it provides the stability and continuity that allow business as usual to proceed. Trumpeting the truth about post-truth from the rooftops might have the effect of destabilizing practices we want to keep in good-running order. Fuller is inclined to bear that cost because he finds it less troubling than the cost in innovation and progress that in his view attends the reign of guardians and gatekeepers.

Fuller is less interested in critiquing or combating post-truth than he is in understanding its history and its function in the present scene. He stands to the side of that large majority of critics for whom the post-truth condition is an occasion for lament and a stimulus to remedial action. These Chicken Littles write in the spirit of the Oxford English Dictionary definition of post-truth (the substitution of emotion for fact-finding) and look around for contemporary sources of what they see as the post-truth epidemic, along with its prime precipitation, fake news. They speak of the rise of "an unhealthy relativism." They contrast the deployment of emotion and story to "the cool assessment of verifiable evidence."

some moral truths. The idea of an "unhealthy relativism" that spreads like a virus through every aspect of your life and leads you to commit acts of betrayal and mendacity is based on a mistake, the mistake of thinking that your philosophical views (should you have any, and most people don't) determine your daily behavior. I don't mean to say that there are no real-world relativist positions. The First Amendment is itself one, for in its strongest form the amendment refuses to distinguish between low and high or important speech and negligible speech. All instances of speech deserve its protection and must be regarded as equal items in an indeterminate mix. That's relativism if anything is.

Relativist arguments are often countered by pointing to so-called indisputable facts. The idea that facts can persuade by themselves so long as an audience's mind has not been clouded by emotional appeals was put forward by Aristotle in his *Rhetoric* and immediately repudiated in the same paragraph.[33] Perhaps in an ideal world, a world in which people were by nature impartial and without ego-driven interests, facts alone (if there were such a category) could prevail. However, in our world, where we are all too human, success in disputation depends on the skillful deployment of the rhetorical skills Aristotle would like to disdain but cannot, owing, he says, "to the defects of our hearers." Logos (Aristotle's term for a bare recital of the facts) won't do it; ethos (Aristotle's term for the advantage you gain by presenting yourself as a good person) must be added, as must pathos (the art of speaking to your audience's desires and prejudices). However much we might desire an unmediated encounter with fact, mediation in the form of personal and political appeals will always be a feature of our attempts to know the truth.

This does not mean, as Matthew d'Ancona charges, that speaking truth has been written out of the job description for politicians; it was never written in in the first place if by "truth" you mean the unvarnished, pure truth as opposed to the truth that emerges in the course of debate. Politics as an activity exists because the default condition of human beings is not agreement but difference. Each of us has a different understanding of what the world is like and what should be done to improve it. When we speak in a public forum for a candidate or a policy, the truths we announce are truths given by the point of view we occupy, and the truths proclaimed by our opponents are truths given from the point of view *they* occupy. Speaking the truth is what everyone claims (and claims sincerely) to be doing, and politics is the game of sorting those claims out in the legislature and at the ballot box.

It follows, then, that facts, rather than being *subordinate* to political views, as Lee McIntyre, a research fellow at Boston University, complains they are, come along with political views. If you see the world through a strongly political lens, if you are a conservative or a liberal or a libertarian or an anarchist, the "facts" of the world you live in will appear in the shape that lens delivers. If, for example, you believe that men and women are capable of lifting themselves up by their bootstraps even when the circumstances of their birth are unpromising, the weakness of many to do that will be seen by you as a culpable weakness of will; they just weren't up to it and that's a fact. But if you believe that circumstances severely limit what men and women can do and that those who rise above their circumstances are near miraculous exceptions, you will think that government should extend a helping hand to the disadvantaged, and the word "disadvantaged" will be for you a fact while your political opposite will regard it as an excuse. (*These people just won't get off their rear ends.*) Political battles are not fought over the stable and self-identifying body of fact; they are fought for the right and authority to specify, at least for a time, what the facts are.

That is why, despite Moynihan's catchy aphorism, you *are* entitled to your own facts if you can make your version of them stick.

Moynihan assumes that fact and opinion come clearly labeled and that the distinction is stable and clear enough for any rational person to see. But in fact (a phrase I don't shrink from) the establishment of fact occurs when some opinion is urged so effectively that it finds a place in the roster of facts accepted, or at least deemed plausible, by the relevant institutions and populations. Facts, in short, are opinions that have made it; facts emerge from the crucible of argument. One could say, then, that "alternative facts" (Kellyanne Conway's infamous phrase) are opinions in waiting, opinions that have not yet gone mainstream, but could if the conditions were right. President Trump and his then press secretary, Sean Spicer, were derided when they claimed that the crowd gathered for Trump's inauguration in 2017 was the largest in history. For mainstream commentators this claimed "fact" was falsified by the simple act of counting. But there are other ways to think about the matter. Suppose that the calculation of crowd size were made in relation to the weather or to the other events competing for the public's attention in a given year but not every year or to the relative number of Democrats and Republicans in Washington or by some other measure claimed to be more sophisticated than the counting of noses. One could then do a statistical analysis within the parameters of that measure and conclude that Trump's crowd was indeed the largest. Now before you get mad at me, let me say that I am not making any such argument, merely observing how it could be made in a manner not wholly ridiculous or easily dismissible. Trump himself showed how it is done when, in response to a reporter's pointing out that he had not in fact received the biggest electoral victory since Ronald Reagan, as he had claimed, he replied, "I was talking about Republicans." When the same reporter challenged *that* statement by referencing the landslide victory of George H. W. Bush, Trump said, "I was given that information," but then immediately added, "[I]t was a very substantial victory, it is the (pejorative) name of the way things are always seen, from an angle. When McIntyre says that "all ideologies are an enemy of the process by which truth is discovered,"[36] he implicitly offers a recipe for discovering it: just divest yourself of all ideological affiliations—political, religious, economic, etc.—and consider the matter, whatever it is, with clear and unbiased eyes. Unfortunately the recipe cannot be followed. Ideology is the label we give to beliefs that are not ours (just as hate speech is the name we give to views we despise); everyone has an ideology because everyone has beliefs.

So what is being recommended when you are told to distance yourself from ideology is that you suspend your beliefs on the way to being a responsible participant in the democratic process. But the recommendation does not come with a set of directions; you're never told how to do it. In fact, you can't. You can't step to the side of your beliefs on the way to acquiring a clearer vision; you can only step from one belief to another, and at every point what you saw would be a function of your belief. If you did some-how manage the impossible and emptied yourself of all beliefs, there would be no "you" that could now see clearly. Beliefs are not entities we think with; they are what we think *within*; they do not stand to the side of consciousness where they can be easily discarded or changed; they are the content of our consciousness, and rather than being obstacles to truth's discovery are the only available route to it. No beliefs, no thought, no judgment, and no self. There is a fallback-halfway position that says we should divest ourselves of slanted beliefs but keep the spot-on ones. But they're all slanted; that's what beliefs are, perspectives within which the world appears, and the project of doing without them or of win-nowing the good ones from the bad ones is a nonstarter because there is no position to the side of belief from whose vantage point the winnowing can be done.

Blame It on Postmodernism (Again)

That's the lesson of postmodernism. The basic postmodernist thesis is that our access to the world is never direct but is mediated by
deeply held assumptions, political and cultural perspectives, disciplinary vocabularies, in-place paradigms—in short by the variable
and changing categories of cognition that inform and shape our
perception and understanding. This condition of never enjoying
an unmediated relationship to Reality with a capital R has not
been visited upon us recently by a gang of French philosophers;
it has been our condition all along. Postmodernism is at most a
report on it, not the cause of it. So it makes no sense to blame
postmodernism for something that predated its appearance in the
world as a set of arguments with a name. That's point 1. Point 2 is
that those who do blame postmodernism for the post-truth condition and everything else often give an account of it that is skewed
or just plain wrong. The book reviewer and cultural critic Michiko
Kakutani announced, in her 2018 book, *The Death of Truth*, that
"postmodernist arguments deny an objective reality existing independently from human perception."[37] No, what postmodernist
arguments deny is the possibility of objectively describing a reality
that is certainly there but is never delivered to us in its own form by
the descriptive methods available to us, methods *we* have ourselves
devised. The philosopher Richard Rorty makes the relevant point
concisely: "[T]he World is out there, but descriptions of the world
are not."[38] Descriptions, he explains, are made up of language, and
"languages are human creations." The world does not identify for
us the language with which we should delineate it. "The world
does not speak. Only we do." And when we speak, what we say is
always at a distance from the referent our words seek to capture.

This does not mean that the choice of which vocabulary to

employ is arbitrary or subjective. Indeed, what postmodernism teaches us is that it couldn't be, for the freestanding self, capable of creating its own reality or conjuring up its own facts, is another of postmodernism's casualties. The self no less than the world it cannot directly apprehend is a product of the beliefs, assumed values, categories of understanding that fill and configure it (the "it" has no stable, essential form), and therefore when Kakutani says that "postmodernism enshrined the principle of subjectivity," she has it exactly backward. If anything, postmodernism undermines the principle of subjectivity.

Matthew d'Ancona, a fellow postmodernism basher, asserts that "the epistemology of Post-Truth," by which he means postmodernism, "urges us to accept that there are 'incommensurable realities' and that prudent conduct consists in choosing sides rather than evaluating evidence." *His* evidence for that judgment is another statement of Rorty's: "Truth is what my colleagues will let me get away with." D'Ancona doesn't quite catch on to Rorty's deadpan comic delivery and his habit of wrapping a complicated argument in what appears to be a throwaway line. The colleagues Rorty refers to are his fellow philosophers, and what he is saying (and my gloss will be infinitely more cumbersome and prosaic than his witty remark) is that any proposition he offers will immediately be vetted and perhaps challenged by his peers. It will then be his responsibility to respond to the challenge in the terms recognized and demanded by the discipline. If he does that successfully and his proposition is accorded a place at the table—it is recognized as a truth claim one can responsibly make even if it does not compel assent from everyone—his colleagues will have let him "get away with" it, at least provisionally. His proposition will have been evaluated and evidence for it will have been required and offered. Hardly a make-it-up-as-you-go or let's-say-anything-we-like process. Once again the point is that postmodernism does not undermine notions of truth, reality, evidence, or objectivity—Rorty was fond of saying "[O]bjectivity is the kind of thing we do around here"—but gives a different account of them, an account less reassuring than the one most of us grew up with, but an account that cannot fairly be characterized as basely political or nihilistic.

McIntyre does no better than d'Ancona or Kakutani when he asks, "[I]f there is no truth and it's all perspective, how can we really ever know anything?"[39] The better question would be, if there were no perspective, how could truth be something we could either know or fail to know? Detached from perspective, from some assumption about the way things are, our minds would have no direction and no way of reasoning from A to B. Without belief and perspective there would be no mental activity. It is only within perspectives—within deeply embedded assumptions about what is out there—that we can set out to determine the truth of a matter or even specify what that matter is. Of course, not everyone proceeds within the same perspective, and that is why, as Kuhn says in *The Structure of Scientific Revolutions*, persuasion, the skill of bringing others around to your point of view, is finally the only route to conviction. It is through persuasion, not disinterested observation, that truth and fact can be established.

Good and Bad Post-Truthers

Persuasion, however, is not an end one achieves just by wishing it or declaring it. It is the product of work, and that work, in order to be successful, must follow certain appointed routes, routes that have authority and force even in a post-truth world. A post-truth world does not lack standards; it just lacks standards that can be securely traced back to a deity or a universal principle or a brute material reality. The fact of a post-truth condition—a condition in which truth has receded behind mediating curtains—has no consequences for the way we know and validate things. It is too general a thesis for that. All it says is that our calculations of truth and fact do not rest on a substratum of bedrock fact. It does not say that our calculations rest on nothing. You can't go from the assertion that unmediated truth is unavailable to us to the declaration that we can say and do anything we like and there is no such thing as a lie. What is and is not a lie is determined by reference to the in-place standards of evidence prevailing in a discipline or practice. Those standards are fashioned in history by men and women—they did not come to us from on high—and they can and do change at varying rates in various disciplines. But as long as they are in force, and some set of them always will be, they provide a basis for making the distinctions we want and need to make: *this is true, this is false, this still is in doubt.* In a world where absolutely objective truth is forever eluding our grasp, conclusions drawn from the structures of validation currently established are all we have, and for most purposes they are good enough.

There is, then, nothing ominous or deeply distressing that follows from the observation that we live, and have always lived, in a post-truth world. What is distressing is the spectacle of some inhabitants of that world (many would point to Donald Trump) acting as if the truth of post-truth is a license to deceive and manipulate because nothing, they believe, can be invoked as a counterweight to whatever they might want to say or do. What can, and should, be invoked are the authoritative (although not God-sponsored) institutions we have painfully built through the centuries, the institutions of philosophy, morality, science, higher education, record-keeping, journalism, etc. The fact that such institutions and the methods they deliver to us are stand-ins for the more objectively grounded ones we can never have in this vale of tears doesn't mean that they are to be discarded or scorned. Rather it means that we must attend to them, refurbish them, and refine them because nothing else will save us (at least not in this life), and if we relax our hold on them or they on us we will indeed court the abyss so many believe is already ours. Those who do not join us in this necessary project, but instead subvert it, mock it, play with it, are bad post-truthers; they surrender gleefully and self-interestedly to the lack of bedrock moorings and celebrate the play of their own imaginations and desires. Cynicism, not postmodernism, is the destroyer of fact and truth; it undermines the trust—provisional, but trust nevertheless—we must have in our honest efforts, the efforts of good and responsible post-truthers, to get things right.

In sum, then:

1. We have always been in a post-truth condition.

2. What that condition deprives us of is the possibility of testing assertions and agendas against a standard of un-mediated truth.

3. In the absence of such a standard we must rely on those standards—not transcendent, but manufactured by humans in time—developed by generations, indeed centuries of intellectual, political, and ethical practitioners.

4. The task of at once maintaining and refining those standards is one engaged in by all responsible persons.

5. Those who abandon that task in favor of various forms of self-interest are post-truthers like the rest of us, but they are bad post-truthers; in Harry Frankfurt's vocabulary, they are bullshitters.

The Post-Truth President

That's the rap against Donald Trump: he is not, many believe, committed to the task of maintaining and refining our standards, but instead plays with them and exploits them, either self-consciously or instinctively. He is a bad post-truther. In the 2016 election both the Democratic and Republican establishments were anti-Trump because they intuitively knew that he was an equal opportunity subverter of everyone's agenda. The leaders of both parties were playing by the same rules and more or less agreed about what one does and doesn't do or say even when they disagreed about policy. But Trump didn't play by the rules. Instead, as news anchor Chris Matthews put it, "Trump always does the opposite of what the rules call for."[40] He changes the game as he plays it, to the consternation of those who are still playing the old game, or trying to. He was at this from the very beginning. When at the first debate of Republican presidential contenders Fox News commentator Megyn Kelly took Trump to task for calling women fat pigs, dogs, slobs, and disgusting animals, there were, according to the conventional playbook, any number of tried and true responses he might have made: he could have denied saying such reprehensible things and complained that he was misquoted or quoted out of context; he could have claimed that he said them in jest; he could have acknowledged that he said them in anger and that he regretted it; he could have announced that he was a changed man and that an earlier Donald Trump misspoke in ways he now repudiated. But Trump did none of these things. Instead he interrupted Kelly, telling her that he applied those derogatory terms only to Rosie O'Donnell—he immediately did the thing he was being accused of—and then he said defiantly, "What I say is what I say." In the next few days, he went on the offensive, calling

Kelly a bimbo and a lightweight and speculating as to what part of her body was leaking blood. His opponents were horrified and piously excoriated him, but they should have recognized that they were dealing with something new and different and recalibrated their strategy accordingly. (Don't ask me what that strategy should have been; so far, no one has been able to answer that question.) Instead they invoked the rules of the game Trump wasn't playing, condemned him, and demanded an apology. He doubled down, retreated not an inch, and watched his poll numbers rise and his opponents drop out.

What Trump knew is what a British Brexiteer knew when he declared that the English people were tired of experts, tired of being told by talking heads with advanced degrees, fancy positions, and fancier addresses what the truth is and what they must believe lest they be labeled ignoramuses or a basket of deplorables.[41] Trump knew that the post-truth sensibility—which means not the abandonment of truth but the refusal to accept it as packaged by so-called experts who are forever quoting each other—had always been lurking in the background and had now come front and center with his campaign. When Trump says, "I know more about Isis than the generals," or when he disdains intensive briefings from experts on the eve of a summit, he is talking, breathing, and performing post-truthness. And because he has become the spokesperson for those who believe that they are smart enough to understand their situation without deferring to PhDs, four-star generals, and so-called public intellectuals, any invocation by his opponents of traditional, pre-post-truth authorities (which are themselves post-truth in the strict sense; they are manufactured rather than transcendent) will fall on deaf ears. Whatever you might think about Trump, there can be no doubt that he speaks powerfully to those who feel scorned by a self-anointed elite. Calling Trump the first post-truth president, rather than being a criticism, could easily be a compliment for his being in touch with the mood of the times and knowing how to play it. (Of course this compliment needn't be extended to the content of his policies; he could be good at doing something bad.)

Trump's critics often mock him and deny that he is a skilled political practitioner. It's all ad hoc, they say; there's no method to his madness. But there is. It is the method of "principled irresponsibility," of irresponsibility raised to a political art form. Most public figures are aware of what they said yesterday or last week or last month, and they become nervous and defensive when someone accuses them of inconsistency. They are eager to tell a coherent story about themselves and their actions, even if the story they tell rarely succeeds in papering over the cracks and fissures in the record. Trump doesn't even try, for his concern is not to exhibit a link between what he said and did at various points in time, but to say or do the thing that will best serve his purpose (usually the purpose of looking good) at *this* point in time. We are often advised to live in the present; Trump really does it. He feels no responsibility to consecutive thought; his words are responsible only to the public-relations urgency of the present instant and have no extended life to which he might be held accountable. Trump-world is created anew at every moment, and when his words have served the moment, they just die and fade away, leaving him entirely free to do it again and again in a future that is always untethered to any past. Trump's critics make the mistake of arguing with him, as if arguments—propositions related to one another in a sequence—are what he is presenting. No, he is presenting postures, postures calculated to get him off the hook *now*. What happens later just isn't in his picture, and it's not in the picture of those who hang on his every perfectly irresponsible word. Until his opponents catch on to this and stop trying to catch him up or catch him out—as they repeatedly do to no discernible effect—they will never come up with a way of beating him at a game he entirely owns.

The only person who seemed to get the better of Trump was Special Counsel Robert Mueller, and he did it by paying no attention to him (at least in public) and saying nothing. Mueller's resolute silence—he went about his business without letting anyone peek into the machinery of his inquiries—put Trump in the position he likes to put others in, trying to get a fix on someone who refuses to present a stable target. Trump does this by being radically unstable and unpredictable; you can't attack him, you can only react to him, and therefore you are always one step behind him. Mueller did the same thing by remaining behind the curtain of an investigation whose shape Trump could only guess at and sputter about. Mueller was as frustrating to Trump as he was to the opponents who couldn't lay a glove on him even when his lies, indiscretions, and possible crimes were entirely out in the open for all to see. Here, then, is a strategy Trump's opponents might adopt: say nothing about him, and just take care of business. But the strategy is one politicians are unlikely to embrace since they are addicted to having their say, and once they do that, Trump is again in the driver's seat.

Is There Something to Be Done about the Post-Truth Condition?

Is there *any* way to play the game better than Trump does? Can post-truth strategies be countered or outflanked? These questions are taken up by those who see both Trump and the post-truth condition as regrettable and preventable phenomena with a twin source in bad motives and bad philosophy and think they can be stopped. What do these anti-post-truthers advise? For the most part, their advice is almost comically feeble. Kakutani says that we should "defy the cynicism and resignation that autocrats and power-hungry politicians depend on."[42] But "defy" is a marching order without content; it's whistling in the dark. McIntyre, in a similar vain vein, declares that "one always must fight back against lies."[43] Right, but how? We might begin, he says, by remembering that according to "empirical evidence," the "repetition of true facts eventually does have an effect." This amounts to proposing that we fight fire with fire: if they are saturating the internet and other media venues with false facts, we must respond with cluster bombs of true facts. Note, first, that this strategy surrenders to post-truth's key thesis—the unavailability of facts that speak for themselves— and counsels a war of our facts against theirs, where victory will be won by sheer numbers. Note also that an accelerated battle of competing facts is unlikely to clarify much for the target audience; it will only confuse its members and further convince them that it's all bullshit. D'Ancona sees this and declares that "facts are not enough." In order to "defend the Truth against the President," we will have to fashion "powerful counter-narratives";[44] in short, we will have to tell better stories. It hardly needs saying that this recommendation is an even more obvious surrender to post-truth rather than a way of combating it. (I am not criticizing d'Ancona and his fellow hand-wringers for telling partisan-inspired stories. What else can they do?)

Another of McIntyre's recommendations for fighting back is undermined by evidence he himself provides. He spends a great deal of time documenting the cognitive biases, which he says "are just part of the way that our brains are wired": confirmation bias (the tendency to give credence to assertions that confirm our preexisting beliefs), bias resulting from an overestimation of our abilities, biases so strong that the presentation of counter-information only makes them stronger. But don't despair, says McIntyre, for "[o]nce we are aware of our cognitive biases, we are in a better position to subvert them."[45] But with what part of our brain would we be aware? And how does that part of the brain, if it could be located, escape the cognitive biases McIntyre lists? His mistake is to think that awareness is a separate muscle of the mind that can be flexed and brought in to break the spell of particular contexts. Awareness is something we experience *within* contexts, and its content is always context-specific. If I am a "sports junkie" watching a game, I'm likely to be aware of the subtle strategies a less obsessed spectator would miss. If I've watched thousands of movies in my time, I'm likely to be aware how indebted one of them is to previous films and see that indebtedness as a message being sent by the director, a message a casual viewer would miss. So while awareness names a level of attention we can achieve in our practices, those same practices will dictate and limit the form awareness can take. Awareness is always a particular, not a general mental condition. It can't be coherently recommended as a cure for anything.

D'Ancona has still another candidate for a sure way to "detect all or most falsehoods in real time." It is something, he says, we don't yet have but will have, perhaps, in the future: "a fully developed Artificial Intelligence" that would have built into it "a sensitivity to linguistic nuance, insinuation, emotional content and apparent intent." (This, you will recall, is Zuckerberg's remedy for the depredations of hate speech.) I get it! A machine programmed by us will be able to make distinctions we ourselves are unable to make, presumably because the massive data banks it can survey in an instant will reveal patterns of behavior that wear their moral status—truth-speaking or post-truth-fabricating—on their face. This is a persistent dream, the dream that procedures from which the human factor has been removed can improve human judgment. Forget about it; it will never happen.

So what to do? Well, what we can't do is return to a pre-post-truth condition where facts were perspicuous and honored and falsehood withered in the light of day in obedience to Justice Brandeis's dictum. We can't return to those days because they never existed. That is the first lesson to be learned about post-truth: it names not a recent unfortunate condition but the condition of being human, not gods. To the extent that they rely on the recovery of a state of clear seeing that has never existed except in Eden, the remedies proposed by those lamenting the post-truth condition are not worth the breath it takes to utter them. These remedies aim too high; they are after a general solution to the problem (if it is a problem), when only local efforts will work or have a chance of working. You dislike Trump and believe that his policies are disastrous? Labor to defeat him in the next election by playing the game more smartly than those who have not yet figured out what they're up against have managed to do. Sick of lies and outrageous conspiracy theories that proliferate daily? Pass laws that will penalize those disseminating verbal poison (at least as you see it), and don't flinch when the First Amendment is brandished as a weapon against you. In short, do what you always do when a situation seems so bad that you fear for the health of the enterprise: roll up your sleeves, marshal the resources available to you, and go out and smite them hip and thigh. Will you succeed? Will it be the case, as d'Ancona proclaims in the last sentence of his book, that "[t]he truth will out"? No, if the truth invoked is *the* truth as it exists apart from our discursive practices, for to that truth we have no access. But we do have access to the truths that emerge in the wake of our collaborative and honest efforts to figure out what we should do, and those truths will "out" if we persevere in the task.

I leave the last word on fake news and post-truth to the Roman satirist Juvenal and the British man of letters Samuel Johnson. In his third satire, Juvenal's friend Umbricius, who is leaving Rome, pauses at the gates of the city to hurl invectives at its citizens. His cry is "What can I do at Rome" where no one follows an honest calling? Everyone lies. Everyone contrives to turn black into white. Everyone is an expert in flattery, and flatterers, not honest men, are believed. Nothing is sacred. People shamelessly do shameful things. They pretend to care but are only playacting. Umbricius obviously could go on forever in this vein, but, he observes, the "sun is sloping" and it's time to go. "So farewell." Many centuries later Samuel Johnson writes in imitation of Juvenal's poem. He substitutes London for Rome, but the sad song is the same. The speaker is eager to leave behind those who

> vote a patriot [John McCain?] black and a courtier [Paul Manafort?] white;
> Explain their country's dear-bought rights away,
> And plead for pirates [Vladimir Putin?] in the face of day;
> With slavish tenets taint our poison'd youth
> And lend a lie the confidence of truth.[46]

The laments for the triumph of post-truth are forever being renewed, and in every society there are those who hold out hope that we can escape, either materially or psychologically, to some better place—not Rome, not London, not Washington or New York—where truth is truth and lies are lies and the news is real and reliable. If you find it, let me know.

CHAPTER 6

Epilogue, or What Does It All Mean?

So now that we've engaged in a quick forced march through some complicated and convoluted First Amendment territory, what can we take away? Well, at first glance the takeaway (or conclusion) is largely negative, a list of things you won't find no matter how hard you look for them.

- You won't find a free-speech principle that unifies and makes sense of First Amendment jurisprudence. All you will find are particular issues in relation to which it has been thought useful to invoke First Amendment slogans (like the Marketplace of Ideas) and distinctions (like the speech/action distinction) that will not hold up under scrutiny but are perfectly usable (and, indeed, necessary) nevertheless.

- You won't find a way to identify hate speech as a category whose members are uncontroversial. All you will find are utterances regarded as hateful or hurtful by some persons, and the class of those utterances includes everything that has ever been said, something Oliver Wendell Holmes saw early on when he declared that every idea is an incitement to somebody.[1]

• You won't find a campus landscape chock-full of free-speech controversies. All you will find are disputes about professional boundaries and administrative responsibilities dressed up as disputes about freedom of speech. Free-speech doctrine, rather than clarifying campus issues, often obscures them.

• You won't find a way of reconciling the Religion Clause of the First Amendment with a Constitution that insists on the equality of all forms of speech. All you will find is the wholly unstable jurisprudence produced by the anomaly of a clause that singles out religion for special attention.

• You won't find a formula for distinguishing between fake news and real news. All you will find is news that emanates from a variety of perspectives and no way of distinguishing between them now that trust in traditional institutions has been eroded by a wave of populism on the one hand and a messianic faith in data on the other.

• You won't find an explanation of how we came to be living in a post-truth era because we have always been living in a post-truth era, in an era when truth, rather than preexisting debate and argument, is the product of debate and argument. And if we've always been living in a post-truth era, you won't find a way of escaping it either by returning to an Edenic past or by moving into a future cleansed of distortions and lies.

• And you won't find a surefire way to delegitimate the presidency of Donald Trump, if that's what you're after. What you will find, and what has always been available in situations of political distress, are the ready-to-hand strategies of partisan politics, which guarantee no outcomes but hold out at least the hope that the outcomes you desire might be achieved.

Now it might seem that the conclusion to be drawn from this list of what you won't find is that the search for the will-o'-the-wisps it names—a free-speech principle, the speech/action distinction, hate speech, a coherent Religion Clause, real news, real truth—should be abandoned and that we should proceed with our eyes open and without the false aid of these fabrications. That would be exactly the wrong conclusion, for they are fabrications only with reference to entities that are *not* fabricated. And if, as I have been arguing, there are no such entities, fabrications—human inventions devised to perform certain tasks—are all we have, and it is imperative that we maintain them. The fact that the speech/action distinction cannot be cashed in and is infinitely malleable (as the case law abundantly shows) is no reason to discard it; it makes possible all of the ingenious maneuvers First Amendment jurisprudence so abundantly displays when there is a job to be done. The fact that all news is fake news (at least with respect to the demand for perfect accuracy) does not mean that we should throw up our hands and surrender to the flood of undifferentiated narratives; it means that we must try all the harder to advance the narratives we find persuasive and might prove persuasive to those who read and listen to us. Real news is news reported by those whose aspiration it is to be faithful to fact; not success in that aspiration but *having* that aspiration is what distinguishes the real from the fake. The fact that the post-truth condition has always been and will always be ours doesn't mean that we give up on truth, but that we nourish and support the institutions—the press, universities, professional associations, documentary films, encyclopedias, the Library of Congress, the *Congressional Record*, the Bureau of Labor Statistics, the Census Bureau—that are dedicated to its pursuit, a pursuit that will never be completely successful but one that can yield tentative conclusions and rules of thumb that allow us to continue with a provisional certainty. If nothing firmer than their own histories and traditions uphold the institutions we inhabit and rely on, we cannot assume that they will take care of themselves. We must commit ourselves to their maintenance and possible improvement, even if our efforts to do so find no anchor in eternity.

We must start, says philosopher Simon Blackburn, "where we are, and deal with problems as they arise, deploying a huge inheritance of mental habits, experiences, natural and practiced capacities of observation, and inference and reasoning."[2] That "huge inheritance" is at once substantial and fragile, for there are always those who wish to take it away from us either by casting aspersions on it or by inundating it with rivers of doubt. Should they succeed—a possibility that cannot be discounted—we would be in perilous waters indeed because, as Blackburn reminds us, "[w]e cannot live without elementary confidences [and] cemented routes of inferences," routes cemented not by Nature or God but by ourselves. The historian and sociologist Steven Shapin explains that this is true even of science. No one, he points out, does experiments from scratch; one must proceed down the paths laid out by others and trust in what they have established: "[W]henever experiments are performed and the results of empirical engagement with the world are reported and assessed, this is done within some system in which trust has been reposed and background knowledge taken for granted."[3] Distrust does occur, but, says Shapin, it is "something which takes place on the *margins* of trusting systems." Were distrust to be insinuated into the heart of those systems, we would be in the grip of a wholesale skepticism where *nothing* was taken for granted, and we would have succeeded (if that is the word) "in knowing nothing at all." The routes to knowledge and fact we have fashioned rest only on their own foundations, but that is precisely why we must preserve them even as we try always to perfect them.

In his great essay "Force of Law" the philosopher Jacques Derrida deconstructs everything in sight and especially the concept of justice, which, he says, is always escaping our efforts to capture it in the form of the laws that are on the books. Justice, he says, always "exceeds law"; no procedures and definitions, no matter how rigorous and detailed, can deliver justice to us; it cannot be assessed or measured; it is "incalculable"; that is, we cannot proceed from some general axiom to deduce its required form in particular circumstances.[4] And yet the very unavailability of justice—like the unavailability of real news or objective truth or a free-speech principle—requires us to persist in our attempts to be answerable to its demands even if we cannot be sure of what they are. "And so incalculable justice requires us to calculate" (*La justice incalculable commande donc de calculer*). It is only by ever refining the calculations we have hazarded, even when we know that they are radically ungrounded, that we can go "beyond the place we find ourselves" to some other place we cannot now imagine and can only hope to reach in the future. Nothing, Derrida declares, "seems . . . less outdated than the classical emancipatory ideal"—the ideal of proceeding step by step in the direction of a just world by casting off error after error—and he says that after having dismantled the resources traditionally thought to be the routes to realizing that ideal.

Derrida calls us to progressive and emancipatory action not despite the absence of a firm ground for its achievement but *because* of the absence of that ground. Were there a firm ground, our labors could be relaxed without consequence, because that ground would always be there even if we lost sight of it temporarily. But if it never appears to us, no matter how strenuous our efforts to apprehend it, we have no recourse but to keep moving forward in the hope that someday it will reveal itself. It may seem paradoxical, but the prerequisite for persevering in our quest for truth, justice, transparency, fact, real news, and the perfect form of democracy is to acknowledge, without flinching, that none of these is available to us this side of eternity, except in the shapes we imperfectly—that is, humanly—come to know through our incessant labors.

ACKNOWLEDGMENTS

For the third time, Julia Cheiffetz gave a book of mine its title (blame for the subtitle lies with me) and didn't let me off the hook until I produced something accessible to an audience beyond my small circle of friends. Julia was ably seconded by Caitie Hawthorne and Mark LaFlaur, who did their expert part in making the manuscript better than it was when they received it. I owe debts I cannot catalogue to those friends and colleagues who read and commented on innumerable drafts: Larry Alexander, William Araiza, Ulrich Baer, Richard Brooks, Lenny Davis, Peter Goodrich, Gerald Graff, Tom Joyce, Josh Pashman, Michael Stokes Paulsen, Michael Robertson, Richard Sander, Frederick Schauer, Steve Smith, Barbara Hernnstein Smith, and Jane Tompkins. None of this would have been possible without the superb help of Megan Labgold and Chelsea Pietrzak, who unfailingly responded to my distress calls even at odd hours.

NOTES

CHAPTER 1: Why Censorship Is a Precondition of Free Speech

1. Tim Wu, "Is the First Amendment Obsolete?," in *The Free Speech Century*, ed. Lee C. Bollinger and Geoffrey Stone (Oxford: Oxford University Press, 2018).
2. Janus v. American Federation of State, County, and Municipal Employees, Council 31, et al., 138 S. Ct. 2448 (2018).
3. West Virginia State Board of Education v. Barnette, 319 U.S. 624 (1943).
4. Texas v. Johnson, 491 U.S. 397 (1989); Chaplinsky v. New Hampshire, 315 U.S. 568 (1942).
5. Whitney v. California, 274 U.S. 357 (1927); John Milton, *Areopagitica* (1644).
6. Deepa Bharath, "Facebook CEO Mark Zuckerberg's Comments about Holocaust Deniers Spurs Free Speech Debate," *Los Angeles Daily News*, July 23, 2018, https://www.dailynews.com/2018/07/20/facebook-ceo-mark-zuckerbergs-comments-about-holocaust-deniers-spurs-free-speech-debate/; Katie Reilly, "Mark Zuckerberg Says He Didn't Intend to Defend Holocaust Deniers in a Recent Interview," *Time*, July 18, 2018, http://time.com/5342383/mark-zuckerberg-holocaust-denial/.
7. Bhikhu Parekh, "Is There a Case for Banning Hate Speech?," in *The Content and Context of Hate Speech*, ed. Michael Herz and Peter Molnar (New York: Cambridge University Press, 2012).
8. Adam Liptak, "How Conservatives Weaponized the First Amendment," *New York Times*, July 1, 2018, national edition.
9. Catharine A. MacKinnon, "The First Amendment: An Equality Reading,"

in *The Free Speech Century*, ed. Lee C. Bollinger and Geoffrey R. Stone (New York: Oxford University Press, 2019).

10. Citizens United v. Federal Elections Commission, 558 U.S. 310 (2010).

11. Judith Butler, "Ruled Out: Vocabularies of the Censor," in *Censorship and Silencing*, ed. Robert Post (Los Angeles: Getty Research Institute for the History of Art and the Humanities, 1991).

12. Sue Curry Jansen, *Censorship: The Knot That Binds Power and Knowledge* (New York: Oxford University Press, 1991).

13. Aja Romano, "Google Has Fired the Engineer Whose Anti-diversity Memo Reflects a Divided Tech Culture," *Vox*, August 8, 2017, https://www.vox.com /identities/2017/8/8/16106728/google-fired-engineer-anti-diversity-memo.

14. Fredrick Schauer, "First Amendment Opportunism," in *Eternally Vigilant: Free Speech in the Modern Era*, ed. Lee Bollinger and Geoffrey Stone (Chicago: University of Chicago Press, 2002).

15. Virginia State Board of Pharmacy v. Virginia Citizens Consumer Counsel, Inc., 425 U.S. 748 (1976).

16. Larry Alexander, *Is There a Right to Freedom of Expression?* (New York: Cambridge University Press, 2005).

17. Robert Post, "Recuperating the First Amendment Doctrine," in *Censorship and Silencing*, ed. Robert Post (Los Angeles: Getty Research Institute for the History of Art and the Humanities, 1991).

18. United States v. Dennis et al., 194 F.2d 201 (2d Cir. 1950).

19. Collin v. Smith, 578 F.2d 1197 (7th Cir. 1978).

20. Glenn Greenwald, "Conservatives, Democrats, and the Convenience of Denouncing Free Speech," *Guardian*, September 16, 2012, https://www .theguardian.com/commentisfree/2012/sep/16/conservatives-democrats -free-speech-muslims.

21. McCullen v. Coakley, 573 U.S. 464 (2014).

22. Chaplinsky v. New Hampshire, 315 U.S. 568 (1942).

23. New York Times v. Sullivan, 376 U.S. 254 (1964).

24. Gertz v. Robert Welch, Inc., 418 U.S. 323 (1974).

25. 1 Cor. 13:12.

26. Timothy Garton Ash, *Free Speech: Ten Principles for a Connected World* (New Haven: Yale University Press, 2016).

27. Jürgen Habermas offers a version of this strategy when he defines the "ideal speech situation" as one in which participants offer only "the better argu-

ments." See Habermas, *Legitimation Crisis* (1973; Boston: Beacon Press, 1975).

28. Rudolf Carnap, *The Logical Structure of the World* (1928).

CHAPTER 2: Why Hate Speech Cannot Be Defined

1. Collin v. Smith, 578 F.2d 1197 (7th Cir. 1978).
2. Donald Alexander Downs, *Nazis in Skokie: Freedom, Community, and the First Amendment* (Notre Dame, IN: University of Notre Dame Press, 1985).
3. Gitlow v. New York, 268 U.S. 652 (1925).
4. Carl Auerbach, "The Communist Control Act of 1954," *University of Chicago Law Review*, no. 23 (1956).
5. UN General Assembly, "Universal Declaration of Human Rights," Article 19 (1948).
6. UN General Assembly, "International Covenant on Civil and Political Rights," Article 22.2 (1966).
7. Miklos Haraszti, "Foreword: Hate Speech and the Coming Death of International Standards before It Was Born (Complaints of a Watchdog)," in *The Content and Context of Hate Speech*, ed. Michael Herz and Peter Molnar (New York: Cambridge University Press, 2012).
8. Arthur Jacobson and Bernhard Schlink, "Hate Speech and Self Restraint," in *The Content and Context of Hate Speech*, ed. Michael Herz and Peter Molnar (New York: Cambridge University Press, 2012).
9. "'Disgusted' Officials File Complaint Against Man in Anti-Immigrant Rant," Liz Robbins, *New York Times,* May 17, 2018.
10. Jeremy Waldron, *The Harm in Hate Speech* (Cambridge, MA: Harvard University Press, 2012).
11. Nadine Strossen with John K. Wilson, "An Interview with Nadine Strossen," in *The Content and Context of Hate Speech*, ed. Michael Herz and Peter Molnar (New York: Cambridge University Press, 2012).
12. Waldron, *The Harm in Hate Speech*.
13. Mitch Landrieu, "We Can't Walk Away from This Truth," *Atlantic,* May 23, 2017.
14. Waldron, *The Harm in Hate Speech*.
15. Waldron, *The Harm in Hate Speech*.

16. Catharine MacKinnon, "Pornography as Defamation and Discrimination," *Boston University Law Review*, no. 71 (1991).

17. Waldron, *The Harm in Hate Speech*.

18. Catharine MacKinnon, *Only Words* (Cambridge, MA: Harvard University Press, 1993).

19. Brandenburg v. Ohio, 395 U.S. 444 (1969).

20. MacKinnon, *Only Words*, p. 13.

21. Waldron, *The Harm in Hate Speech*.

22. Edwin C. Baker, "Hate Speech," in *The Content and Context of Hate Speech*, ed. Michael Herz and Peter Molnar (New York: Cambridge University Press, 2012).

23. Cantwell v. Connecticut, 310 U.S. 296 (1940).

24. Abrams v. United States, 250 U.S. 616 (1919).

25. Frederick Schauer, *Free Speech: A Philosophical Enquiry* (New York: Cambridge University Press, 1982).

26. Richard Delgado, "Words That Wound," *Harvard Civil Rights–Civil Liberties Law Review*, no. 17 (1982).

27. *Darkest Hour*, directed by Joe Wright (2017).

28. Snyder v. Phelps, 562 U.S. 445 (2011).

29. Cohen v. California, 403 U.S. 15 (1971).

30. See James Thomas and Sander Gilman, *Are Racists Crazy?* (New York: New York University Press, 2016).

31. Viktor Mayer-Schönberger and Teree E. Foster, "More Speech, Less Noise: Amplifying Content-Based Speech Regulations through Binding International Law," *Boston College International and Comparative Law Review*, no. 18 (1995).

32. Mill, *On Liberty*.

33. Alon Harel, "Hate Speech and Comprehensive Forms of Life," in *The Content and Context of Hate Speech*, ed. Michael Herz and Peter Molnar (New York: Cambridge University Press, 2012).

34. Robert Post, "Interview with Robert Post," in *The Content and Context of Hate Speech*, ed. Michael Herz and Peter Molnar (New York: Cambridge University Press, 2012).

35. Eric Heinze, *Hate Speech and Democratic Citizenship* (New York: Oxford University Press, 2016).

36. Eric Heinze, "The Case against Hate Speech Bans," *Eurozine*, April 9, 2014, https://www.eurozine.com/the-case-against-hate-speech-bans/.

37. Louis Brandeis, "What Publicity Can Do," in *Other People's Money and How Bankers Use It* (1914); Whitney v. California, 274 U.S. 357 (1927).

38. Brian Leiter, "The Case against Free Speech," *University of Chicago Law School Journal Articles*, no. 8662 (2016).

CHAPTER 3: Why Freedom of Speech Is Not an Academic Value

1. Katherine Mangan, "Trump Says He'll Sign Order Requiring Colleges to Protect Free Speech," *Chronicle of Higher Education* online, March 2, 2019, https://www.chronicle.com/article/Trump-Says-He-ll-Sign-Order/245812.

2. Geoffrey R. Stone, "Free Speech on Campus: A Report from the University Faculty Committee," January 6, 2015, University of Chicago Law School, https://www.law.uchicago.edu/news/free-speech-campus-report-university -faculty-committee.

3. Keith Whittington, *Speak Freely: Why Universities Must Defend Free Speech* (Princeton: Princeton University Press, 2018).

4. But see Princeton University v. Schmid, 455 US 100 (1982) for an argument that would bring a private university within the ambit of the First Amendment.

5. American Association of University Professors, "1915 Declaration of Principles on Academic Freedom and Academic Tenure" (1915).

6. Prudence Carter and R. Jay Wallace, report to Chancellor Carol Christ, University of California, Berkeley, April 10, 2018.

7. Robert Post, "There Is No 1st Amendment Right to Speak on a College Campus," *Vox*, December 31, 2017, https://www.vox.com/the-big-idea/2017/10 /25/16526442/first-amendment-college-campuses-milo-spencer-protests.

8. Erwin Chemerinsky and Howard Gillman, *Free Speech on Campus* (New Haven: Yale University Press, 2017).

9. Post, "There Is No 1st Amendment Right to Speak on a College Campus."

10. Erwin Chemerinsky, "Hate Speech Is Protected Speech, Even on College Campuses," *Vox*, December 26, 2017, https://www.vox.com/the-big-idea /2017/10/25/16524832/campus-free-speech-first-amendment-protest.

11. "Middlebury College professor injured by protesters as she escorted controversial speaker," March 6, 2017, *Addison Independent* (Middlebury, Vermont), https://www.addisonindependent.com/201703middlebury-college-professor -injured-protesters-she-escorted-controversial-speaker.

12. Herbert Marcuse, *Repressive Tolerance* (Boston: Beacon Press, 1965).

13. Mark Bray, "Trump and Everyday Anti-Fascism beyond Punching Nazis," *Roar*, January 23, 2017, https://roarmag.org/essays/trump-everyday-anti-fascism/.

14. Whittington, *Speak Freely*.

15. Conor Friedersdorf, "In Defense of Harvey Weinstein's Harvard Lawyer," *Atlantic*, March 3, 2019; Randall Kennedy, "When a Dean Defends Harvey Weinstein," *Chronicle of Higher Education*, February 28, 2019.

16. Derald Wing Sue, *Microaggressions in Everyday Life* (Hoboken, NJ: Wiley, 2010).

17. I have appropriated (intellectually, not culturally) arguments Walter Benn Michaels has been making for twenty years. See *Our America* (1997), "The Myth of Cultural Appropriation," *Chronicle of Higher Education*, July 2, 2017. Lionel Shriver, speaking at the Brisbane Writers Festival in 2016, insisted that, taken seriously, the ban on cultural appropriation made novel writing impossible, at least for authors who invented characters far from their own experience.

18. Greg Lukianoff and Jonathan Haidt, *The Coddling of the American Mind: How Good Intentions and Bad Ideas Are Setting Up a Generation for Failure* (New York: Penguin, 2018).

19. Chris Bodenner, "The Surprising Revolt at the Most Liberal College in the Country," *Atlantic*, November 2, 2017, https://www.theatlantic.com/education/archive/2017/11/the-surprising-revolt-at-reed/544682/.

20. Ulrich Baer, *What Snowflakes Get Right* (Oxford: Oxford University Press, 2019).

21. Chloe Maxmin, "A Generation's Call: Voices from the Student Fossil Fuel Divestment Movement," *Dissent*, April 9, 2014.

22. Drew Gilpin Faust, "Fossil Fuel Divestment Statement," October 3, 2013, Harvard University, https://www.harvard.edu/president/news/2013/fossil-fuel-divestment-statement.

23. American Association of University Professors, "1915 Declaration of Principles on Academic Freedom and Academic Tenure" (1915).

24. Amy Wax and Larry Alexander, "Paying the Price for Breakdown of the Country's Bourgeois Culture," *Inquirer*, August 9, 2017, https://www.philly.com/philly/opinion/commentary/paying-the-price-for-breakdown-of-the-countrys-bourgeois-culture-20170809.html.

25. "How should a Dean who understands academic freedom respond to public

controversy about faculty writing?" September 29, 2017, *Brian Leiter's Law School Reports* (blog), https://leiterlawschool.typepad.com/leiter/2017/09/how-should-a-dean-who-understands-academic-freedom-respond-to-public-controversy-about-faculty-writi.html.

26. Guest column by thirty-three Penn Law faculty members, "Open Letter to the University of Pennsylvania Community," *Daily Pennsylvanian*, August 30, 2017, https://www.thedp.com/article/2017/08/guest-column-by-33-penn-law-faculty-members-open-letter-to-the-university-of-pennsylvania-community.

27. Penn National Lawyers Guild, "Penn NLG Statement on Professor Amy Wax," August 25, 2017, National Lawyers Guild, Penn Law Chapter, https://nlgpennlaw.wordpress.com. In July 2019, Wax raised hackles again when she was reported to have said at a conference of conservatives that this country "would be better off with more whites and fewer non-whites." Taken by itself this remark would appear to be racist, but behind it is an argument Wax recently made in an article in which she made the case for what she calls "cultural distance nationalism," a nationalism based on the conviction that a "large influx of immigrants from nations that do not share our cultural values and understandings, will undermine citizen morale, unity, and solidarity as well as the integrity of our institutions" (Amy L. Wax, "Debating Immigration Restriction: The Case for Low and Slow," *Georgetown Journal of Law & Public Policy* [2018]). "Cultural distance" nationalists believe that immigration policies should favor people who are "more like us." The result will be that more whites than nonwhites will be admitted to the country, but Wax contends that this follows from a cultural preference, not a racial one. It is hardly surprising that her view has been roundly condemned. See Zack Beauchamp, "Trump and the dead end of conservative nationalism," *Vox*, July 17, 2019.

28. Guest column by Dean of Penn Law School Ted Ruger, "On Charlottesville, Free Speech and Diversity," *Daily Pennsylvanian*, August 14, 2017, https://www.thedp.com/article/2017/08/guest-column-dean-ted-ruger-penn-law-charlottesville-amy-wax.

29. Lucy Curits, "Amy Wax's New Op-ed Rekindles Old Debate in Penn Law," *Daily Pennsylvanian*, February 26, 2018, https://issuu.com/dailypenn/docs/0226_e545c3c617a808.

30. Guest Column by Brown U. Prof. Glenn Loury, "Reflections on My Interview with Amy Wax," *Daily Pennsylvanian*, March 27, 2017, https://

www.thedp.com/article/2018/03/guest-column-amy-wax-glenn-loury -affirmative-action-penn-law-african-american-ruger-upenn.

31. Amy L. Wax, "The University of Denial," *Wall Street Journal,* March 22, 2018, https://www.wsj.com/articles/the-university-of-denial-1521760098.

32. Theodore Ruger, "Dean Disputes White Professor's Statements on Black Students," Associated Press, March 14, 2018, https://www.apnews.com /20124d385bac4fe1a428fe50316eb417.

33. Derek Hawkins quoting Theodore Ruger, "Penn Law Professor Who Said Black Students Are 'Rarely' in Top Half of Class Loses Teaching Duties," *Washington Post,* March 15, 2108.

34. "Penn Trustee Emeritus resigns over University 'treatment of Amy Wax,'" Sarah Fortinsky, *Daily Pennsylvanian,* April 9, 2018, https://www.thedp .com/article/2018/04/amy-wax-board-of-trustees-paul-levy-penn-law-upenn -pennsylvania-upenn-gutmann-resignation.

35. Steven Salaita, Twitter post, July 8, 2014, 10:46 p.m., https://twitter .com/stevesalaita/status/486718092933099520; Steven Salaita, Twitter post, July 19, 2014, 7:24 p.m., https://twitter.com/stevesalaita/status /490683700116738048.

36. University of Illinois Urbana-Champaign Senate, "Concerns about Shared Governance and Academic Freedom," approved March 9, 2015, https://www .senate.illinois.edu/rs1507.pdf.

37. Scott Jaschik, "The Emails on Salaita," *Inside Higher Ed,* August 25, 2014, https://www.insidehighered.com/news/2014/08/25/u-illinois-officials-defend -decision-deny-job-scholar-documents-show-lobbying.

38. James Tracy, "FAU Professor Questions Whether Sandy Hook Massacre Was Staged," *South Florida Sun Sentinel,* December 15, 2015.

39. James Tracey, "Disclaimer," *Memory Hole Blog,* https://memoryholeblog.org /disclaimer/.

40. Mary Jane Saunders, email message to Florida Atlantic University, January 10, 2013.

41. Patricia McGuire, "How Colleges Should Deal with Their Kellyannes," *Chronicle of Higher Education,* August 29, 2018, https://www.chronicle.com /article/How-Colleges-Should-Deal-With/244388.

42. Historians Against Trump, "An Open Letter to the American People," July 11, 2016, https://historiansagainsttrump.org/2016/07/an-open-letter-to-american -people.html.

43. Janet Napolitano, "It's Cruel: Janet Napolitano on Trump's 'Zero Tolerance' Policy," *Politico: Women Rule*, podcast audio, June 20, 2018, https://itunes.apple.com/us/podcast/women-rule/id1210928141?mt=2.

44. Nell Boeschenstein, "An Open Letter to My Fellow Teachers on the Weekend after the Election of Donald Trump," *Guernica*, November 17, 2016, https://www.guernicamag.com/an-open-letter-to-my-fellow-teachers-on-the-weekend-after-the-election-of-donald-trump/.

45. Robert A. Blouin, email message to deans of Chapel Hill, December 6, 2018.

46. Paula McMahon, "Jury Rules against Fired FAU Prof James Tracy in Free Speech Case," *South Florida Sun Sentinel*, December 11, 2015.

47. Mitchell Langbert, "Kavanaugh: A Modest Proposal," blog, September 27, 2018, http://mitchell-langbert.blogspot.com/2018/09/kavanaugh.html.

48. Conor Fridersdorf quoting Jeannie Suk Gersen, "In Defense of Harvey Weinstein's Harvard Lawyer," *Atlantic*, March 3, 2019. In early May 2019, the Harvard administration announced that Sullivan and his wife, Stephanie, would not be continuing as faculty deans. The Harvard College dean said that the decision was informed by "a number of considerations." Shortly before the announcement of his nonrenewal, Sullivan resigned from the Weinstein defense team, citing conflicts with his teaching obligations. See Kate Taylor, "Harvard's First Black Faculty Deans Let Go," *New York Times*, May 11, 2019.

49. Donald Trump, speech at CPAC Convention, March 2, 2019.

50. See the website of the University of Minnesota, Office of the Executive Vice President and Provost: https://provost.umn.edu.

51. Tinker v. Des Moines Independent Community School District, 393 U.S. 503 (1969); Pickering v. Board of Education, 391 U.S. 563 (1968); Connick v. Myers, 461 U.S. 138 (1983); Garcetti v. Ceballos, 547 U.S. 410 (2006).

CHAPTER 4: Why the Religion Clause of the First Amendment Doesn't Belong in the Constitution

1. Reynolds v. United States, 98 U.S. 145 (1879).

2. Everson v. Board of Education, 330 U.S. 1 (1947).

3. Gen. 22:2.

4. United States v. Seeger, 380 U.S. 163 (1965); Welsh v. United States, 398 U.S. 333 (1970).

5. United States v. Seeger, 380 U.S. 163 (1965).

6. Michael Stokes Paulsen, "Is Religious Freedom Irrational?," *Michigan Law Review,* no. 112 (2014).

7. Lynch v. Donnelly, 465 U.S. 668 (1984).

8. County of Allegheny v. American Civil Liberties Union, Greater Pittsburgh Chapter, 492 U.S. 573 (1989).

9. Marsh v. Chambers, 463 U.S. 783 (1983).

10. Elk Grove Unified School District v. Newdow, 542 U.S. 1 (2004).

11. John Locke, "A Letter concerning Toleration" (1689).

12. Cécile Laborde, *Liberalism's Religion* (Cambridge, MA: Harvard University Press, 2017).

13. Engel v. Vitale, 370 U.S. 421 (1962); Santa Fe Independent School District v. Doe, 530 U.S. 290 (2000).

14. Laborde, *Liberalism's Religion.*

15. Obergefell v. Hodges, 135 S. Ct. 2584 (2015).

16. Obergefell v. Hodges (6th Cir. 2014).

17. Katherine Franke, "Law Professor: Davis Can't Evoke Religion to Deny Marriage Licenses," interview by Robert Siegel, *NPR,* September 1, 2015.

18. Noah Feldman, "Commentary: The choice for Kim Davis: Serve the public or resign," in *Chicago Tribune*, September 3, 2015, https://www.chicagotribune.com/opinion/commentary/ct-kim-davis-kentucky-clerk-gay-marriages-20150903-story.html.

19. West Virginia State Board of Education v. Barnette, 319 U.S. 624 (1943); Wooley v. Maynard, 430 U.S. 705 (1977).

20. Elane Photography, LLC v. Willock, 572 U.S. 1046 (2014).

21. See Axson-Flynn v. Johnson, 356 F.3d 1277 (10th Cir. 2004).

22. Church of the Lukumi Babalu Aye, Inc. v. City of Hialeah, 508 U.S. 520 (1993).

23. Employment Division, Department of Human Resources of Oregon v. Smith, 494 U.S. 872 (1990).

24. Craig v. Masterpiece Cakeshop, Inc., COA 115 (2105).

25. Church of Lukumi Babalu Aye v. City of Hialeah, 508 U.S. 520 (1993).

26. Hosanna-Tabor Evangelical Lutheran Church and School v. EEOC, 132 S. CT. 694 (2012).

27. Burwell v. Hobby Lobby Stores, Inc., 134 S. Ct. 2751 (2014).

28. Masterpiece Cakeshop, Ltd. v. Colorado Civil Rights Commission, 138 S. Ct. 1719 (2018).

29. "Colorado, baker end legal spat over transgender woman's cake," Kathleen Foody, Associated Press, March 5, 2019, https://www.apnews.com/88f528e624c34cf 384c238b857ee4a72

30. Sarah Murray, "The Owner of Red Hen Explains Why She Asked Sarah Huckabee Sanders to Leave," *Washington Post*, June 25, 2018.

31. Laborde, *Liberalism's Religion*.

32. Garton Ash, *Free Speech*.

33. Ira C. Lupu and Robert W. Tuttle, "The Limits of Equal Liberty as a Theory of Religious Freedom," *Texas Law Review*, no. 235 (2007).

34. Laborde, *Liberalism's Religion*.

35. Susanna Mancini and Michel Rosenfeld, introduction to *The Conscience Wars: Rethinking the Balance between Religion, Identity, and Equality*, ed. Susana Mancini and Michel Rosenfeld (New York: Cambridge University Press, 2018).

36. Robert Post, "The Politics of Religion," in *The Conscience Wars: Rethinking the Balance between Religion, Identity, and Equality*, ed. Susana Mancini and Michael Rosenfeld (New York: Cambridge University Press, 2018).

37. Richard Dawkins, *The God Delusion* (London: Bantam Press, 2006); Sam Harris, *The End of Faith: Religion, Terror, and the Future of Reason* (New York: W. W. Norton & Co., 2005); Christopher Hitchens, *God Is Not Great: How Religion Poisons Everything* (New York: Twelve/Hachette Book Group, 2007).

38. Snyder v. Phelps, 562 U.S. 443 (2011).

39. United States v. Stevens, 559 U.S. 460 (2010).

40. Citizens United v. Federal Elections Commission, 558 U.S. 310 (2010).

41. See Stanley Fish, "Our Faith in Letting It All Hang Out," *New York Times*, February 12, 2006. https://www.nytimes.com/2006/02/12/opinion/our-faith-in -letting-it-all-hang-out.html.

42. Garton Ash, *Free Speech*.

CHAPTER 5: Why Transparency Is the Mother of Fake News

1. David E. Pozen, "Transparency's Ideological Drift," *Yale Law Journal*, no. 128 (2018).

2. Max Farrand, ed., *Records of the Federal Convention of 1787* (New Haven: Yale University Press, 1966).

3. Lawrence Lessig, "Against Transparency," *New Republic,* October 9, 2009, https://newrepublic.com/article/70097/against-transparency.

4. Archon Fung, Mary Graham, and David Weil, *Full Disclosure: The Perils and Promise of Transparency* (Cambridge, UK: Cambridge University Press, 2007).

5. Evgeny Morozov, *To Save Everything, Click Here: The Folly of Technological Solutionism* (New York: Public Affairs, 2013).

6. Mark Zuckerberg, keynote address at SXSW, March 9, 2008.

7. Victor Davis Hanson, "Fake News: Postmodernism by Another Name," *Defining Ideas: A Hoover Institution Journal,* January 26, 2017.

8. Harry G. Frankfurt, *On Bullshit* (Princeton: Princeton University Press, 2005).

9. Mark Fenster, *The Transparency Fix: Secrets, Leaks, and Uncontrollable Government Information* (Stanford: Stanford University Press, 2017).

10. Pozen, "Transparency's Ideological Drift."

11. Omri Ben-Shahar and Carl E. Schneider, *More Than You Wanted to Know: The Failure of Mandated Disclosure* (Princeton: Princeton University Press, 2014).

12. Wu, "Is the First Amendment Obsolete?"

13. Francis Fukuyama, "The Limits of Transparency," *American Interest,* January 4, 2015, https://www.the-american-interest.com/2015/01/04/the-limits-of-transparency/.

14. Søren Kierkegaard, *Journals and Papers* (1848).

15. Hubert L. Dreyfus, "Kierkegaard on the Information Highway," UC Berkeley Art, Technology, and Culture Colloquium, October 15, 1997, https://goldberg.berkeley.edu/lecs/kierkegaard.html.

16. Daniel J. Solove, "Speech, Privacy, and the Internet," in *The Offensive Internet: Speech, Privacy, and Reputation,* ed. Saul Levmore and Martha Nussbaum (Cambridge, MA: Harvard University Press, 2010).

17. Matthew d'Ancona, *Post-Truth: The New War on Truth and How to Fight Back* (London: Ebury Press, 2017).

18. Testimony to Congress of Mark Zuckerberg, April 11, 2018, *Washington Post* YouTube channel.

19. Jerry Z. Muller, *The Tyranny of Metrics* (Princeton: Princeton University Press, 2018).

20. Angie Schmitt, "Self-Driving Car Makers Prepare to Blame 'Jaywalkers,'" *Streets Blog USA,* August 17, 2018, https://usa.streetsblog.org/2018/08/17/if-self-driving-cars-cant-detect-jaywalkers-they-shouldnt-be-on-the-roads/.

21. Yoon Lee, "Moving from A.I. to Artificial Wisdom," *Masters of Data*, podcast audio, November 5, 2018.

22. Brittan Heller, "What Mark Zuckerberg Gets Wrong—and Right—about Hate Speech," *Wired*, May 2, 2018, https://www.wired.com/story/what-mark-zuckerberg-gets-wrongand-rightabout-hate-speech/.

23. Steven Johnson, "Why Cloudflare Let an Extremist Stronghold Burn," *Wired*, January 16, 2018, https://www.wired.com/story/free-speech-issue-cloudflare/.

24. Wu, "Is the First Amendment Obsolete?"

25. Kara Swisher, "I Thought the Web Would Stop Hate, Not Spread It," *New York Times*, October 30, 2018, https://www.nytimes.com/2018/10/30/opinion/cesar-sayoc-robert-bowers-social-media.html.

26. Brian Stelter, Jack Dorsey interview, CNN, August 19, 2018.

27. John Perry Barlow, "A Declaration of the Independence of Cyberspace," Electric Frontier Foundation, February 8, 1996, https://www.eff.org/cyberspace-independence.

28. Steve Fuller, *Post-Truth* (New York: Anthem Press, 2018).

29. Thomas Kuhn, *The Structure of Scientific Revolutions* (Chicago: University of Chicago Press, 1962).

30. D'Ancona, *Post-Truth*.

31. Lee McIntyre, *Post-Truth* (Cambridge, MA: MIT Press, 2018).

32. D'Ancona, *Post-Truth*.

33. See Aristotle, *The Art of Rhetoric*. Translation, introduction, and notes by H. C. Lawson-Tancred. London: Penguin Classics, 1991.

34. "Trump Falsely Claims Biggest Electoral Win Since Reagan," William Cummings, *USA Today*, February 16, 2017, https://www.usatoday.com/story/news/politics/onpolitics/2017/02/16/trump-falsely-claims-biggest-electoral-win-since-reagan/98002648/

35. See Cicero, *On Invention [De Inventione]*. Translation by H. M. Hubbell. (Cambridge, MA: Harvard University Press / Loeb Classical Library, 1949).

36. McIntyre, *Post-Truth*.

37. Michiko Kakutani, *The Death of Truth* (New York: Tim Duggan Books, 2018).

38. Richard Rorty, *Contingency, Irony, and Solidarity* (New York: Cambridge University Press, 1989).

39. McIntyre, *Post-Truth*.

40. *Hardball with Chris Matthews*, MSNBC, June 7, 2018.

41. "'People in this country have had enough of experts': Brexit and the para-doxes of populism," John Clarke and Janet Newman, *Critical Policy Studies*, January 28, 2017.

42. Kakutani, *The Death of Truth*.

43. McIntyre, *Post-Truth*.

44. D'Ancona, *Post-Truth*.

45. McIntyre, *Post-Truth*.

46. Samuel Johnson, *London* (1748).

CHAPTER 6: Epilogue, or What Does It All Mean?

1. Gitlow v. New York, 268 US 652 (1925).

2. Simon Blackburn, *On Truth* (New York: Oxford University Press, 2018).

3. Steven Shapin, *A Social History of Truth* (Chicago: University of Chicago Press, 1995).

4. Jacques Derrida, "Force of Law," *Cardozo Law Review*, no. 11 (1990).

INDEX

ABOUT THE AUTHOR

Stanley Fish is the visiting Floersheimer Distinguished Professor of Law at Yeshiva University's Benjamin N. Cardozo School of Law in New York City and the Davidson-Kahn Distinguished University Professor and a professor of law at Florida International University. He has previously taught at the University of California at Berkeley, Johns Hopkins University, Duke University, and the University of Illinois at Chicago, where he was the dean of the College of Liberal Arts and Sciences. He has received many honors and awards, including being named the Chicagoan of the Year for Culture. He resides in Andes, New York; New York City; and Highland Beach, Florida, with his wife, Jane Tompkins.